The Elements
of Rhetoric

The Elements of Rhetoric

VINCENT RYAN RUGGIERO

Department of English
State University of New York, Delhi

PRENTICE-HALL, INC., Englewood Cliffs, New Jersey

© 1971 by PRENTICE-HALL, INC.
Englewood Cliffs, New Jersey

All rights reserved. No part of this book may be reproduced in any form or by any means without permission in writing from the publisher.

Printed in the United States of America

C-13-271916-9
P-13-271908-8

Library of Congress Catalog Card No.: 70-137894

Current printing (last digit):
10   9   8   7   6   5   4   3   2

PRENTICE-HALL INTERNATIONAL, INC., London
PRENTICE-HALL OF AUSTRALIA, PTY. LTD., Sydney
PRENTICE-HALL OF CANADA, LTD., Toronto
PRENTICE-HALL OF INDIA PRIVATE LIMITED, New Delhi
PRENTICE-HALL OF JAPAN, INC., Tokyo

To

Michele
Gail
Teresa
Francis
Michael
Timothy
John
Gerald

and especially to

Lois

with love

Contents

3

4

Preface

To the Instructor

During the past decade many composition instructors have found the traditional rhetoric textbook, with its complete and lengthy treatment of every major and minor rhetorical concern and numerous exercises accompanying each point, of little use in teaching composition. The worst of its assignments are mechanical. The best become dated long before revision time comes around. Each day's news brings a number of new issues or new developments in current issues more deserving of a student's attention. Its writing assignments are often only remotely related to the real writing situations the student is likely to encounter when the course is over. And it is too large and expensive to be used as a supplement to other materials: if it is adopted at all, it tends to dominate the course.

For a time the little writing guidebooks seemed to answer the needs of the modern student. But more and more instructors have become dissatisfied with these textbooks. Some are not even rhetorics, though they claim to be, but breezy discourses on selected conventions of grammar and usage. Many others lack proportion, assigning more space to the rules of spelling or to the split infinitive than to varieties of assertion or the problem of audience. Where they emphasize contemporary practices, they tend to neglect important traditional concepts. Where they gain brevity, they lose comprehensiveness. Where they address the student in a fresh and lively manner, they often talk down to him, or depreciate the subject of rhetoric, or both. There are logic-oriented rhetorics, of course, but most of these treat logic as a subject unto itself, a matter apart from the writing process, outside the context of other important elements of substance, organization, and style.

Little wonder that more than a few of our colleagues, under the pressure of open admissions policies and the level of student verbal skills those policies suggest, embrace the view that writing instructors have no business evaluating student performance, that all evaluation is arbitrary, that the student's effort to express himself and not the quality of his expression should be the measure of his performance. Less wonder that some writing instructors are publishing articles asking, "Is there any real subject matter to be taught in a composition course?" and "Can composition instructors justify their function?"

Anyone who would answer these questions affirmatively must address the related questions: What is that subject matter? Where can one find it stated briefly in a way that demonstrates it is not arbitrary but has significance to situations beyond the composition classroom? In short, an affirmative answer that is convincing—to ourselves as well as to others—demands the existence of a brief, comprehensive rhetoric, a rhetoric that

Identifies and gives primacy to the most important rhetorical concerns without ignoring other important concerns.

Is based on the practices observable in the best of contemporary writing and yet neither caters to the new because it is new nor rejects the old because it is old.

Avoids both the traditional attitude of "These are the principles because rhetoricians say they are—go and follow them unquestioningly" and the contemporary attitude of "There are no principles—do your own thing."

Presents rhetoric interestingly without bogging down in jargon or esoterica, but also without being cute or gushy.

Helps the student to be weaned from dependence on the instructor's assignments and criticisms and prepares him to create his own writing assignments and be his own critic, but without depreciating the instructor's role.

Can be used effectively with other materials (for example, essay anthologies, novels, newspapers) without upstaging them.

Is relevant enough to other courses—literature, history, the sciences, and social sciences—to be considered as a supplemental text there. (Nothing would better demonstrate to students the relevance of a composition program and the importance of its standards than other departments adopting the rhetoric text as a required supplement and expecting students' writing to meet its standards.)

These are demanding criteria. Perhaps no text, including this one, will ever meet them fully. However, this text is an attempt at meeting them. In addition, its design reflects a number of premises about writing and the teaching of writing:

1. The most valuable skills a person can bring to any writing situation are the ability to reason well and to present his thoughts effectively to his audience. Much of the work of the college student in courses beyond composition, in English and in other fields, can be performed efficiently and well only if he has these skills. Moreover, the most important writing and speaking an educated adult is called upon to do as worker and as citizen depend on them. All writing or speaking which demonstrates a lack of these skills, however well formed it may be in other respects, is essentially ineffective. Therefore, these skills should be the primary focus of the composition course.

2. Most beginning writers in college have never given much consideration to the reasoning process, have never asked very pointedly why they hold the views they do. They lack strategies for dealing fairly with thinking not their own and critically with their own thinking. They are accustomed to taking a stand on issues and defending their positions but unaccustomed to inquiring whether the stand they take is the most reasonable one. They are relatively unaware of how their predispositions, assumptions, "common sense," and simplifications can get in the way of sound reasoning. They know *when* they have made up their minds but not *how* they have done so; more important, they don't know how to *unmake* them. They know how to disagree with others by countering their positions but not how to challenge their own ideas. The composition course should show them how to do these things and give them practice in doing them.

3. Few beginning writers, even very capable ones, have ever considered their readers, nor do they know how to consider them. Most beginning writers write either for themselves—often to experience the pleasure of releasing strong feelings about an issue—or for some vast and vague Everyman ("Hey, you out there—I've got something to say"). But since the act of communication presup-

poses, in most cases, addressing not ourselves or Everyman but some specific audience, the subject of how to know one's audience and how to approach them is of special importance and should be given special attention in the composition course.

4. The traditional breakdown of rheotric into four modes—description, narration, exposition, argument—is not very useful in most writing situations. Few professors in other disciplines (or for that matter in literature) make reference to these modes in their writing assignments. The modes are not very informative—that is, we would have difficulty opening a magazine and pointing to a non-fiction article which was any single one of the four modes. It would be much easier to find examples of articles which were all four of them. Moreover, the terminology of the modes does not explain what we are really doing when we write. No serious non-fiction writer speaks of "doing a piece of description about that flood," or "an article of exposition about the shoe industry," or "an argument for tax reform." He speaks about his ideas, the assertions he believes are reasonable, and the evidence or analysis that supports them. To be sure, he uses description and narration and he surely thinks of them, at least as he is using them.[1] But they are the techniques he uses to support or develop an idea; as such, even when they are the dominant techniques, *they are not what he is doing, but the way he is doing it.* In short, description and narration, along with other techniques of development, must be included in the composition course, but they should not be its main focus.

5. Brief, separate treatment of each of the various points of rhetoric is preferable to a grouping of points into chapters. The former makes the material appear less formidable, invites the student's browsing, and is easier for him to use for reference when he is writing. It also permits the instructor to individualize his teaching, directing the student's attention to the sections he needs to concentrate on, without having the entire class work on those sections. (The numbering of "Other Elements of Rhetoric" and "A Glossary of Grammar and Usage" enables the instructor, at his discretion, to give such directions without lengthy comments.)

6. A textbook that contains exercises and assignments is not only used during the course; it is, at least in the student's mind, "used up." The student may be encouraged to take a different attitude toward his rhetoric textbook—to see it as a reference book, useful not only in the composition course, but also beyond it—if no exercises or assignments are included in it. Accordingly, this text has none. An unusually detailed instructor's manual is available on request. It includes numerous assignments in reasoning and persuasion, with emphasis on contemporary issues, as

[1] Exposition and argument, however, are seldom used today to refer to specific activities. Exposition has come to mean all non-fiction writing; argument, presenting a position on a controversial issue.

well as exercises in some of the other elements of rhetoric. It also suggests various ways of using this text.

To the Student

Rhetoric is the study of effective communication. From the beginning of recorded history men have recognized the advantage of being able to express their thoughts and feelings clearly and appealingly to others. And throughout history few have failed to recognize the power of those whose handling of language commands attention—power over other men, events, and ideas, power to shape the course of human history. A man's unusual ability with words was interpreted by some peoples as a sign that he was favored by the gods; the modern counterpart of that idea is that some people are genetically favored. Both ideas spring from the view of communication as an art. Whenever a person says, "Some people have it in English; others don't" or, "I guess I have no talent for writing," he is expressing the same view. And it is a sound view, as far as it goes: some people are more talented than others in speaking and writing. But that is not the whole truth. If it were, then we would never find a poor speaker or writer achieving competency, or a competent speaker or writer achieving excellence. And yet we do. Communication is indeed an art, but it is also a skill. By learning the elements of rhetoric—the characteristics found in the writing and speaking of those acknowledged as gifted—and by applying what we learn, we can make our writing and speaking more effective.

This book is divided into four main parts. The first two are essays on two of the most important elements of rhetoric, those that more than any others govern the effectiveness of most writing—reasoning and persuasion. Most students have been told for years to think; they have even been told what to think; but few have ever been shown *how* to think. Few, that is, have been treated to an examination of the reasoning process and shown the strategies that can improve the quality of their thinking and help them to analyze issues for themselves. Similarly, few students have been directed to consider the effect of their writing on their audience. They know more or less how to write to please themselves (or to say what they think the teacher wants them to say). But they do not know how to anticipate the reader's reactions and make their presentation more effective with him. This lack of knowledge is especially lamentable because in most writing the writer is addressing someone other than himself.

The third section of the book presents the other important elements of rhetoric. Each of these could, of course, be the subject of a volume. The entries here are designed to introduce the concepts and the way they affect your writing and to give you guidance in applying them. They are grouped under three headings—substance, organization, and style. (If you wish to study some of these further, your library undoubtedly has a number of extended treatments of them.) The fourth section is a glossary. It lists the more common errors in grammar and usage and explains how to avoid them.

This book is designed to be useful not only in the composition course but in any course where writing is required, and in the many writing situations that arise after college. You will, of course, be directed to read parts of it before you write, and perhaps to examine certain sections more closely when your papers are returned. But try not to regard it as something to be left on the shelf until you are told to use it. Refer to it before you write and as you are writing. Browse through it occasionally. Use it as a standard for evaluating the essays and articles you read in newspapers and magazines and as a key to observing how other writers achieve their effects.

As you use this book, remember that a writing instructor can be a very helpful guide, but he cannot *make* anyone a better writer. Only the individual can do that. Some people become excellent, even professional, writers without ever taking a formal course in writing, without ever submitting their writing to someone else for his evaluation and suggestions. They become their own instructors, their own critics. The student in a formal course has an easier job than they: he is assisted by someone who has already learned what he is learning. That is what a composition instructor does—helps a student to help himself. The instructor's aim is to have his students become less and less dependent on his directions and criticism. Real success in a writing course, therefore, lies not just in being able to write "C" quality (or better) papers consistently but, more important, in being able to know whether a piece of writing is effective and why, and in being able to improve that which is ineffective.

Acknowledgments

I wish to express my gratitude to all those who had a part in the making of this book. Special thanks to Mr. Gary Gutchell of Prentice-Hall for encouraging me to write the book, to Miss Mildred Beckwith for preparing the manuscript, to my colleagues in the English Department of Delhi College for their continuing dialogue about rhetoric, and to my family for their patience with me through the hours I spent away from them.

The Elements
of Rhetoric

1

Reasoning

Reasoning is the process of drawing conclusions about perceptions and ideas. Perceptions are sensory impressions—sights, sounds, tastes, touches, smells—registered on our minds and integrated with one another. By the time we develop the ability to reason, our senses have recorded millions of these impressions. Consider, for example, how many impressions we experienced as infants in a few minutes of a single day. We were aware of an unpleasant feeling in our abdomens; we reacted to it, then heard our own crying; we saw the shape of mother hovering over us, experienced our own sudden upward movement and the sensation of giddiness that accompanies movement; soon we smelled the sweetness of powder, tasted the warmth of milk, felt the softness of a blanket.

Only some years later, after we learned to smile and crawl and walk and speak, after we spent thousands of days using our senses and responding in various ways to their messages, did we begin to reason about our perceptions. And even then, new perceptions continued to bombard us, some directly, others indirectly in the symbols of written language which we learned to relate to sensory experience, and which formed a bridge between such experience and abstract concepts.

It is hard to speak meaningfully of the reasoning process without continued reference to perceptions, since the two are so closely intertwined. The quality of our reasoning depends on how accurate our perceptions are, how conscious we are of present sensory impressions, and how effectively we recall relevant past sensory impressions and relate them to present situations. It also depends on our natural capacity for, and our acquired habits of, association.

Yet reasoning is neither the perceptions themselves nor the context in which they occur. Nor is it the act of remembering and making associations—as, for example, when we make the unconscious association, "this shirt is the same color as that which I have learned to call indigo," upon seeing an indigo shirt. Reasoning may be as quick as that association, and it may involve remembering past acts of reasoning. But it is a new movement toward a conclusion, *a conscious inquiry into matters less than obvious, a mental effort to select and judge perceptions themselves or the conclusions that have been drawn from them.*

Broadly considered, the types of inquiry that reasoning makes are the following:

1. What things are ("things" including, as well as objects, persons, places, events, activities, processes, and concepts, individually or in classes)—the range and proportions and interrelationships of their characteristics
2. What things do—their functions
3. Their similarity or dissimilarity to other things
4. How they came to be as they are—their origins and development, the influence of other things on them
5. Their influences on other things
6. What they could be (given certain conditions) or should be
7. Their relative value (including symbolic value)
8. The views men take of them

The Human Context

The context in which reasoning occurs is the human context, the human condition with all its limitations. Each of us is a particular center of consciousness, having begun life with a unique genetic constitution and developed through different experiences. Our syntheses of reality, our habitual ways of reacting to sensory data are peculiarly our own. Everything we experience is transformed in being filtered through our personalities, so that when we are describing some reality, we are describing our view of that reality, but not necessarily the reality itself. Each of us is, in a sense, like one of the six blind men who touched the elephant. The first touched his side and concluded that an elephant is like a wall; the second touched his tusk and concluded, "a spear"; the third, his trunk—"a snake"; the fourth, his leg—"a tree"; the fifth, his ear—"a fan"; the sixth, his tail —"a rope." And they disputed at length over what an elephant was like, each certain of his own conclusion, each mistaken. Similarly, each of us will see an event somewhat differently from the way others perceive it. The sight of a policeman arresting a bearded, long-haired young man will be seen differently by an elderly banker, a criminal lawyer, and another bearded, long-haired young man. A picture of an old steam locomotive in a magazine will very likely be just another steam locomotive to us, but to a retired engineer it is a particular model with certain dimensions, capacities, and limitations.

We might expect that our obvious limitations would make us cautious about assigning too much importance to our own views, and anxious to receive other men's views. But, like the six blind men, we seem reluctant to follow this course. More often we infer that because we can experience things only through our own personalities (and not those of other people), our personal opinions have some transcendent value. That inference accounts for the cry, "It's my opinion," heard so frequently today, and usually delivered with the assurance of a medieval political dissident crying, "Sanctuary!" as he raced through the cathedral door. We speak similarly of what an event means "to me" or what a fictional character's experience means "to him," not just in the sense of exploring the very real personal dimension of reality, but also in the sense of asserting that everything we believe or say is a matter of taste, and therefore not open to dispute.

Is the principal drive in man the drive for pleasure (Freud), the drive for power (Adler), the drive for meaning (Frankl), or some other drive? Have American history books tended to omit proportionate reference to Afro-American achievements? Does the absence of proper nutrition in an infant impede the normal growth of brain cells? Do world population trends give sufficient cause for alarm? In discussing such questions it is common for many of us to begin by saying, "Of course, it all depends on how one views the issue." If pressed to specify what we mean by "it," we would probably reply, "the validity of one's idea," and go no further. The problem is that *the term "validity" can be understood in either a personal or an impersonal sense.* When we say someone's idea has personal validity for him, we are saying no more than that his idea has the force of reality for him. But when we say that his idea has *im*personal validity, we are saying that it is in conformity with the relevant facts. Therefore, we can affirm the personal validity of a person's idea (as we always do if it is sincerely held), and yet deny its *im*personal validity. We can admit that our neighbor's belief that George Washington was scrupulously honest throughout his life has the force of reality for him, and still conclude, as contemporary scholars seem to have concluded, that the idea is a fabrication and is therefore invalid in the *im*personal sense.

If we limit the meaning of "validity" to the personal sense, we are suggesting that there is no standard for measuring opinion other than one's personal preference. Were this so, there would be no logical way to argue with anyone about anything. The brain surgeon could not logically argue with the plumber about the therapeutic efficacy of pre-frontal lobotomy—for the plumber's view, like his, would be unassailable. With personal opinion thus elevated, no one could be fired from his job for poor judgment, it is true, but there would be fewer jobs to begin with. Everyone would be his own doctor, lawyer, historian, linguistic authority, aeronautical engineer—the list is virtually endless. Such an exaltation of opinion ultimately denies not only the importance of facts, but the value of the reasoning process as well. If no view is better than any other, why trouble to become informed about the facts of an issue? Why bother with careful evaluation? If anything we say about an issue is valid in every sense of the word, why take any care about what we say?

There is a certain comfort in holding that our ideas are above challenge. This position does seem to free us from the bondage of having to square our ideas with realities outside our minds. But the comfort is false, the freedom really a new form of slavery in which we are bound by the narrow circumstances of our lives. When we exalt personal opinion we express contentment with our separateness and isolation, and refusal to reach out beyond the narrow confines of familiar or pleasurable truths. Moreover, we lose the distinction between what is so and what we imagine to be so. The former becomes synonymous with the latter. Instead of seeking other men's views, weighing them and our own against whatever facts are available, and thereby making our own view larger and truer, we are satisfied to be one of the blind men exhausting himself in shouting his own little view to the world. There is, of course, no escaping our individuality. We can never be completely free of our limitations in time, space, and viewpoint. Therefore, we will never be able to reach a state of complete objectivity; we will always be, for better or worse, subjective in our view of reality. But we needn't wallow in our limitations; it is possible to reach a higher level of subjectivity, one that *approaches* objectivity. And to do that we need only develop the habit of looking beyond personal validity, which demands no evidence other than the fact that one has an idea, to impersonal validity, which demands evidence, and consciously seek to avoid the most common impediments to sound reasoning.

Impediments to Sound Reasoning

The most common impediments to sound reasoning are predispositions, assumptions, "common sense," and simplifications. We all have a tendency toward each of these. Each is in many ways unobjectionable. Yet each can prevent us from seeking the facts and judging them fairly.

Predispositions. A predisposition is a general inclination to regard something favorably or unfavorably before we encounter or experience it. The conditioning we undergo as we grow and develop —the thousands of direct and indirect experiences we have, and all the connections we make, consciously and unconsciously, among them—leave us with many such inclinations. A youth spent in a quiet home with soft-spoken parents may cause us to regard vigorous argument unfavorably. We may have a slight aversion to tall, fair-haired people because of some unpleasant experience with a tall, fair-haired person in high school. Similarly, for a myriad of reasons—some simple, some complex—we may prefer certain colors, certain sounds and rhythms (in language as well as in music), certain patterns and shapes.

Predispositions do not interfere significantly with our reasoning as long as they do not harden into preconceptions—which are not merely general opinions but firm convictions about persons, places, or things we have not yet encountered. Even though they may be accurate, preconceptions tend to prevent reasoning by substituting prejudgment for judgment. When one's general aversion to com-

munists because of ideological differences is escalated to the preconception that every communist is illogical and dishonest in his
handling of historical fact, he is not prepared to listen open-mindedly
to a particular communist lecturer. When a juror has a preconception of welfare recipients as necessarily lazy and immoral he
will not be likely to judge fairly a particular welfare recipient on
trial for theft.

Nor are affirmative preconceptions any better than negative ones.
The news analyst who has a preconception of college protestors
as necessarily motivated only by the highest ideals is not likely
to be very objective when he covers a student demonstration. The
person who has a preconception of soldiers in his country's army as
being incapable of robbing, raping, and murdering civilians is not
likely to consider open-mindedly the charge that a group of soldiers
was guilty of such an action.

Whenever we are reasoning, we do well to examine our predispositions to be sure they have not hardened into preconceptions.

Assumptions. An assumption is a premise that one takes for
granted, a short-cut conclusion that closes off inquiry. Some assumptions are warranted, some unwarranted. The student who
assumes he will without question succeed in Chemistry I because
his professor came from his home town is probably assuming too
much. The student who assumes that he will pass the Chemistry
final examination because he has prepared for it carefully, has done
well on every other exam, and has completed all his assignments,
makes a warranted assumption.

The person who argues that "no one has any right to talk about
something unless he has personally experienced it" is assuming with
too little warrant that personal experience is the only valid way of
acquiring knowledge. Must a doctor have cancer in order to talk
about it? Must a marriage counselor be divorced in order to discuss
intelligently the effects of divorce? Must one have experienced
illiteracy as an adult in order to talk about the problem of adult
illiteracy? Similarly, the person who says, "The generation gap
today is caused by the reluctance of adults to deal with young
people in a non-authoritarian way," is assuming (a) that there is a
"gap" between the generations today, (b) that it is best spoken of
as a single phenomenon (he doesn't say "generation gaps"), and
(c) that it has a single cause. Which of these assumptions is warranted? Perhaps all three, perhaps none. But unless he recognizes
that these assumptions are contained in his statement, he is not

likely to inquire whether the "generation gap" is more apparent than real or whether because there are many forms of gaps between the generations, it is misleading to speak as if there were but one, or whether there is a single cause.

It would be correct to say that we needn't be concerned with our warranted assumptions. The problem is that we do not always know which are warranted until we examine them. In some cases we do not even realize that we are making an assumption until we pointedly ask ourselves whether we are. It is best to be inquisitive about our own thinking and to make a constant effort to identify and evaluate our assumptions.

"Common Sense." "Common Sense" is a misleading term. It means nothing more than the insights deriving from everyday experience and therefore open to everyone regardless of the extent and kind of his education. But somehow it is often used unconsciously to mean the infallible wisdom of the masses. When we are tempted to regard it in this manner, we should remember that what is called common sense may be common error or common ignorance. Of course, it may not seem erroneous; it may be a respected position endorsed by the most eminent thinkers of the time. At one time it was common sense that the earth was a several thousand-year-old square body that served as the center of the solar system. It was common sense that man didn't evolve from the animals, and that the cure for various illnesses was the placing of leeches on the neck to drain off excess blood. Not long ago burning witches was a common-sense habit hallowed by tradition in western countries we regard as highly civilized. And today in many parts of the world, men worship various household gods, make potions, practice magic and voodoo, and pander to the most ludicrous superstitions all in the name of common sense.

Among the most direct challenges to "common sense" is the statement of paradox: that is, a statement that appears absurd, but actually expresses an unfamiliar possible truth. A statement of paradox is often used to retain the complex tension between almost-conflicting aspects of a total truth.

Consider, for example, several statements by a skilled user of the paradox, G. K. Chesterton. His observation, "What ruins mankind is the ignorance of the expert," [1] on the surface seems nonsensical, for an expert seems by definition to be informed rather than ig-

---

[1] *William Blake* (London: Gerald Duckworth & Co. Ltd., 1910), p. 58.

norant. But the shock of that line reminds us that being an expert in one sense increases the likelihood of error—for the more one knows, the more complex the realities he explores and the more easily he can err, the more easily his limitations (ignorance) can manifest themselves. Similarly, his "It is not the wild ideals that wreck the world; it is the tame ideals" [2] seems absurd, until we consider that it is the "tame" ideals that help to perpetuate inequalities and injustices. Again, his assertion that "The globe-trotter lives in a smaller world than the peasant" [3] sounds ludicrous until we consider his observation that the globe-trotter's wide travels and experiences with people often make him fragment his knowledge by focusing on the superficial differences between men, whereas the peasant's more vital contact with his smaller universe is always unfragmented and total.

It is unwise to accept or reject an idea merely because it does or doesn't conform to common sense.

Simplifications. It is natural for us to try to simplify the realities we deal with in order to understand and communicate them. Given the complex nature of realities and the limited resources of human language, the human mind seems to be required to grasp in fragments or to reduce large unwieldy realities to manageable size. And the act of communication, spoken or written, demands even greater reduction, compression, and imposed organization for the sake of coherence. Simplification is therefore necessary. We have to live with it and accept it.

But there is a point at which simplification becomes oversimplification, which, unlike simplification, doesn't scale down the reality, retaining its real proportions as far as possible; rather, it blurs or omits proportions altogether. Underlying oversimplification is the attitude that no matter how complex an issue may be, there must be a clear-cut, simple, "pat" answer. A man says, "The democrats' intention is to replace personal responsibility with the dole." This oversimplification distorts. Another says, "People raised during the depression are conservative and cautious because they experienced deprivation." This ignores the fact that some people raised in the depression did not experience deprivation then, and that some who did experience deprivation became reckless as a result. A minister declares, "Young people who don't attend church are too attached to their sinful pleasures," ignoring the fact that there are many

[2] *Heretics* (London: The Bodley Head Limited, 1905), p. 252.
[3] *Ibid.*, p. 49.

possible reasons for young people not attending church. The beginning history student states that the cause of World War II was Hitler's invasion of Poland, ignoring the fact that because there are proximate causes and remote causes, primary, secondary, and tertiary causes, a complicated question like this cannot be answered so simply.

Oversimplification is an impediment to reasoning in that it makes us close our minds to complexity, makes us think we already have the answer we seek. It makes us content with forced superficial explanations that, not unpredictably, often support our prejudices.

Dealing With Contradictions

One of the most helpful starting points for a line of reasoning is the identification of a contradiction. A contradiction is a direct inconsistency or logical opposition between two ideas. It is a signal for us to stop and examine the ideas and decide which is correct. Our basis for refusing to accept contradictions is the principle of contradiction, the rule that *a statement may not be both true and false at the same time and under the same circumstances.* The car you drive cannot *be* a Cadillac and *not be* a Cadillac. If it is a Cadillac, then it is not anything else. If it is not a Cadillac, then it must be something else. It may be a Chevrolet, a Ford, a Jaguar—but it is not a Cadillac if it is not a Cadillac. (The rule is very simple, really. Do not look for it to say more than it does.) Consider the following examples:

1. Two music lovers are talking. The first says, "I really enjoyed that Beethoven selection in last night's concert." The second replies, "There was no Beethoven selection in last night's concert." (Both can't be right. Either may be, but whichever is, the other is wrong.)

2. A doctor and a cigarette manufacturer are arguing. The doctor says, "Smoking is a causative factor in lung cancer." The cigarette manufacturer answers, "Smoking is decidedly *not* a causative factor in lung cancer." (Both can't be right. Either smoking is a factor or it isn't. There may at this time be no conclusive evidence. But we know with certainty that it cannot be a factor and not be a factor at the same time in the same way.)

3. A minister has reached the ultimate impasse in a discussion with an atheist friend. "But I tell you God exists," the minister asserts.

"And I tell you God does not exist," the atheist responds. (If you ever meet a person who claims he is able to accept both these statements at the same time, send him to a psychiatrist. One can believe God exists, or he can disbelieve, or be uncertain as to whether he believes, but he cannot believe and disbelieve at the same time in the same way.) We can say without fear of being contradicted that one of these two statements must be true and that the other must be false.

4. A scientist and a humanist are debating. The scientist asserts that scientific and technological achievements alone can help men live at peace with one another. The humanist answers that alone, scientific and technological achievements cannot ever do so. We can be certain that if one of these men is correct, the other is incorrect.

The point is that in terms of the correctness of any one of these problems, both propositions cannot be equal. If one is correct, the other is necessarily incorrect, because they are mutually contradictory. But the more practical matter which concerns us here is how do we determine which of the statements is true? For the first example our method is relatively simple. We find a copy of the program and examine it to see if a Beethoven selection is listed. Unless there is a question whether all the selections listed were played, or whether some were not listed but added to the program, we will have our answer.

The second is a little more difficult. We will have to consult statistics. In all probability we will find them indicative of an answer but not conclusive. (If you look at the side of the pack of cigarettes you shouldn't have in your pocket but probably do have, you will read "Caution: Cigarette Smoking May Be Hazardous to Your Health." The key words are "May Be," indicating the lack of final proof in the matter.) To arrive at our answer we will therefore have to rely first on statistics and then on reason to interpret them.

For the third problem there are no statistics to consult. There are only experience and reasoning. Most of us find little difficulty in believing in God (if we believe) or in disbelieving (if we disbelieve). Some of us, it is true, have thought very little about the question of God's existence and have merely accepted what we were taught. But most educated men and women have evaluated their childhood beliefs and have based their adult acceptance or rejection of them on reasoning.

The fourth problem, the question of whether science can have the answer to the problems of relations among men, is as difficult as the third. We must rely on reasoning, but reasoning used in a specific way. We must consider the historical achievements of science and decide what types of problems science has proved capable of handling. Then we must consider the methods of science and ask whether the problem of the nature of man can be solved by these methods alone.

Because not every problem in thinking can be approached in exactly the same way, we must first decide what approach is best. We therefore ask: Is there a source we can go to for a conclusive answer? Are there statistics that we can consult? If there are, are they conclusive or must we evaluate them? Does history provide similar situations for our evaluation? Must we reach our conclusion principally or exclusively by reasoning? It is well for us to remember that our reasoning is never so effective as when joined by the reasoning of other men, particularly those whose writings have stood the test of time. It is well also for us to keep in mind that some problems (for example, the fourth one above) may never be fully resolved because of their complexity and because the subjects —science and the relations among men—are themselves changing.

Sometimes when we examine what we believe is a contradiction, we find it is only an apparent contradiction and not a real one. For example, two men are arguing over whether contemporary America is undergoing a revolution. One is saying there is clearly a revolution, the other, that there is no trace of revolution. The impasse seems total. Yet there may be no contradiction at all: it may be that the first man is correct in one sense and the second man in another sense. Without realizing it, the men may be operating with different definitions of "revolution." The first may mean by the term a momentous change in America's values and attitudes. The second may mean the more traditional idea of revolution—violent overthrow of government. It is possible to argue at length over such a matter without realizing that the difficulty is not perceptual, but linguistic. When each comes to understand that the other is assigning "revolution" a different meaning, the path to understanding is cleared. It may lead only to identification of some real conflict, but that is an important achievement.

Unmaking Our Minds

"Make up your mind" is a familiar admonition. It is a pity that "unmake your mind" isn't as familiar. For the fact is we often have our minds made up when we shouldn't have. And sometimes we have them made up wrongly. At the beginning of this century the mass of men were convinced it was ridiculous for man to hope to fly—the first airplanes were the butt of popular humor; people were convinced Jules Verne's stories of voyages to the moon and under the sea would always be idle fantasy; few could believe in the possibility of machines that purify and cool air or that "think" electronically; the idea of a heart or kidney transplant was ridiculous. Between then and now people were forced to unmake their minds about each of these things and hundreds more like them. In addition, many ideas accepted then as literal truths have been shown to be myths—the idea that the white settlers of the American West were always more civilized than the Indians, for example, or the idea that dire poverty has no effect on a person, that his personality and character are not at all conditioned by what he experiences.

To make up our minds on a matter is not just to reach a conclusion about it, but to regard the conclusion as irrevocable. It is to deny the possibility that the conclusion could be even partly mistaken, and to assert that no new knowledge can ever challenge it. Responsible men do not avoid drawing conclusions, but if they are wise, they keep them open to modification and change. For human knowledge is constantly expanding. Today's awareness surpasses yesterday's. Tomorrow's accepted fact may be, with good reason, challenged next week. There is no area of reality about which human understanding is ever fixed, final, complete. For these reasons, our dilemma is that we must evaluate and act without full assurance that what we decide or do is correct. We have no infallible guides. The best we can do is demand that all our judgments and actions be, in light of whatever evidence we have available, as reasonable as we can make them. But how do we evaluate our own positions on particular questions to determine whether they should be modified? How do we unmake our minds? Here are two approaches:

REVERSE THE IDEA

1. Take the exact opposite of our idea.
2. Build the best possible case for this opposite view by jotting down all the evidence that supports it.
3. Compare the original idea with its opposite. Ask if the opposite

is more reasonable. If it is not, ask whether what we have considered about the opposite should make us modify our original view.

If the idea we wished to evaluate were that homosexuals freely choose their sexual preference (that is, that they are willful deviates from human sexual norms), we would reverse it to the idea that homosexuals do *not* choose their sexual preference. Ideas with which we were familiar would not require any research. This one we probably would have to research. An hour or two spent efficiently in the library would produce evidence that the homosexual, like the heterosexual, seldom if ever chooses his sexual character. He discovers it; it happens to him. Thus in comparing the original idea with its reverse we would realize that while some homosexuals may freely choose to accept their sexual impulses and not try to change them, they do not choose to have those impulses rather than heterosexual impulses.

EXTEND THE IDEA

1. Determine the logical, ultimate extension of the idea.
2. Consider what the effects would be on society as a whole or on certain parts of society if everyone accepted and applied the idea in his life.
3. Ask if the effects would be beneficial or detrimental and decide under what conditions, if any, the idea is valid.

Consider, for example, the idea that the way for students to deal with a college administration they believe is not acting in their best interests is to occupy offices, invade classrooms and halt teaching, and prevent other students from using campus facilities. The logical, ultimate extension of the idea would be for everyone who feels aggrieved to act similarly against those who have wronged him. Now since no human enterprise is perfect, every human enterprise will conceivably offend, or seem to offend, someone. What would the effects be in this case? Creameries would be paralyzed and babies would have no milk. Hospitals would be paralyzed, and there would be no care for those whose lives depend on it. The list is endless. Some effects, of course, would be beneficial. The ones who expressed their grievances would derive emotional satisfaction. Certain evils might even be eliminated by the pressure of such protest. But it is not difficult to see that the bad would outweigh the good effects. Therefore, we would judge the original idea at the very least as a serious matter not to be considered lightly, perhaps applicable only in grave situations after other, less disruptive means of protest had failed, and even then with the greatest possible restraint.

Recognizing Our Limitations

In reasoning about complex issues we may avoid committing errors in thinking by being aware of our limitations and sensitive to the most common errors regarding them:

a) *Avoid drawing hasty conclusions, those that do not necessarily follow from the evidence presented.* They may follow, or they may not. It is impossible for us to make a valid judgment without more evidence. The most frequent causes of this error are inadequate study of the evidence and the failure to make necessary distinctions. To avoid or discover hasty conclusions, ask if the evidence supports only the conclusion drawn or if it will as well support a different conclusion. Consider the following passage, written by a student:

> I have noticed that whenever I meet a new situation, I immediately recall similar situations in the past. My reactions now are governed by my reactions then. And since I know that all my experiences are indelibly recorded in my mind, I conclude that a personality develops on past experience, that we are all products of the past, that the past is in fact the determining factor in our future.

The student did present evidence—his own experience. But perhaps because he was so familiar with it, he failed to study it adequately. If he had, he would have questioned whether such complex processes as recall, thought, and action can be summed up so simply, and he would have questioned whether his own experience supports a conclusion about people in general. In addition, although he correctly observed that the past influences the future, he jumped from this observation to the conclusion that because it is a factor, it is therefore the determining factor. Had he said, "Our past is an influencing factor in our future," his conclusion would not be quite so vulnerable to challenge.

Hasty conclusions are frequently found in discussions of cause and effect relationships, especially where two things happen simultaneously, but are not necessarily related. For example, a writer may say:

> The rise in the price of butter in our state last year was clearly an effect of the new farm subsidy policy.

The cautious writer asks himself, as does the cautious reader, "Is the cause and effect relationship real or only apparent? Have I perhaps been deceived by the coincidence of these two happenings? Are they perhaps unrelated?" The test, of course, lies in the evidence presented. If the evidence admits of another conclusion, and if the conclusion offered is not appropriately qualified, the conclusion must be judged hasty.

b) *Recognize what you really know and what you only guess.* You may, for example, hold a position about Freud's theory of sexuality or Darwin's theory of evolution or Marx's theory of class struggle. But have you ever asked yourself in all candidness, "What do I really know about these theories? Have I ever read a single quotation from the writings of these men? Have I ever read a commentary or critical analysis of their ideas? Or have I merely heard their names so often that I have deceived myself into believing that I actually know something about them and their theories?" If you have not had any significant contact with their ideas, you must, if you are honest, suspend your judgment until you have. This is not to say that you may have no opinion about such men's ideas until you have read all, or even a large number, of their works. It is to say that you must appraise your knowledge or lack of it fairly, and keep your opinions appropriately tentative, remaining open to the possibility of modifying your view as you learn more about the subject.

c) *Know when to rely principally on your own experience and when not to.* Some subjects can be handled satisfactorily by presenting just your own experiences and observations. Consider, for example, L. P. Smith's statement, "How awful to reflect that what people say of us is true." You could probably write a very effective composition by relating, with appropriate interpretation, particular incidents you have experienced or witnessed that illustrate the idea. But there are other subjects which you can handle satisfactorily only by going beyond your experiences and observations to those of other writers. If, for example, the subject of your composition was a defense of the idea that the main cause of rioting in urban ghettos is lack of employment opportunities, your experience would be of little value unless it included considerable first-hand contact with the ghetto. You would undoubtedly have to find and present the evidence of social workers, policemen, newspaper and magazine reporters, and experts in the social sciences.

There is no simple, foolproof test we can apply to determine when to rely merely on our own experience. The best we can do is to ask whether our experience will support a statement of any significance. If it will not, we had best ask what we have read and what we might read to provide us with such evidence. It is better to pass over a topic, no matter how inviting it may be to us, if we cannot make and support a worthwhile, though perhaps modest, statement about it or if we haven't the time to spend reading more about it. (For further discussion of this point see *Evidence* in "Other Elements of Rhetoric.")

d) *Know when to say "No" and when to say "Yes, but."* Some positions it is necessary to reject altogether because they are false. Others must be accepted in part, but rejected in part. An example of the first is this sentence from Maine de Biran—"The greatest evil of man is not to know how to direct his life." To this the most appropriate response (in its own terms) is "No. It is rather to know how to direct his life and yet not do it." But the following passage (from a student's composition) cannot be summarily dismissed.

> Dressing the part does not make a boy a juvenile delinquent. If this were so, then every child who put on a cowboy suit would become a cowboy. Every man who put on a business suit would become a businessman. Even more absurd, every boy who dressed as a lion or a tiger at Halloween would become a lion or a tiger. We dress to suit our surroundings. In some areas Ivy League is the mode of dress, and in others it is the leather jacket garb which takes precedence. No, clothes do not make the juvenile delinquent.

There is some truth in this statement. But not the whole truth. The appropriate response here would be the second type, the "Yes, but" response—"Yes, it is true that clothes do not make the delinquent. But they do give him a sense of identity with those he wishes to imitate. They become a symbol, an unconscious association which cannot help but condition his behavior."

e) *Try to determine not only whether the idea is principally true or false, but also the degree of its truth or falsity.* The critical thinker, like the uncritical, will on occasion agree completely with the position of another person. But far more often he will agree in part and disagree in part. This is not because he likes to disagree, but because he recognizes, as the uncritical person does not, how often a statement is mainly true but contains elements, however minor, of falsity. He also realizes how easily one's desire to attack an extreme position can lead him to the opposite extreme.

f) *Be sure to be as critical of an argument for a position you agree with as you are of one for a position you disagree with.* A serious, mature thinker will not hesitate to criticize a poor or superficial argument even if he agrees with the position it is used to support. He knows that such an argument can turn reasonable men away from a position. He is therefore quick to disavow it, openly and forcefully.

Important Distinctions in Reasoning

Of primary importance in dealing with all questions that involve conflicting evidence and opinions is care in making necessary distinctions. The following are perhaps not the only distinctions to be made, but they are the most fundamental:

1. DISTINGUISH BETWEEN WHAT WAS AND WHAT IS.

One observation common to all men is the observation that few things, if any, stay the same. People change, places change, ideals change. The changes may not occur at the same rate, and some places and ideals may resist longer than others, but some type of change at some time is inevitable. This fact bids us guard against assuming that people, places, and ideals are today as they were in the past. They may be, or they may not be. For example, someone might say, "history books indicate that the black man has never reached a high state of civilization." But that person would fail to realize that while history books *did* generally indicate that, they no longer do. For a variety of reasons—some innocent, some perhaps not—historians omitted adequate reference to black civilizations. Today they are repairing those omissions. What was so is no longer so. Whenever you are saying something is so, ask yourself if you are sure it is *still* so.

2. DISTINGUISH BETWEEN WHAT IS AND WHAT CAN BE, WILL BE, SHOULD BE.

Do not assume that what is so is *necessarily* so, that an existing situation cannot be changed or should not be changed. Some would argue, for example, that because poverty in India is so widespread, nothing can be done about it; or that because crime in the United States has increased despite all efforts to combat it, we must accustom ourselves to a growing crime rate; or that because a certain student has never been interested in his school work, all efforts to make him interested will necessarily fail. These people fail to distinguish between *what is* and *what can be*, fail to see that the two are not necessarily identical. Others would argue that because the United States is the richest nation in the world, it will always be the richest nation in the world; or that because Canada is now friendly to us, Canada will always be friendly to us. These fail to distinguish between *what is* and *what will be*. Still others reason that the fact that there is capital punishment implies that there should be capital punishment. They fail to distinguish between *what is* and what *should be*. It is true that sometimes what is is what can be, or what will be, or what should be, *or all three*. But since this is not necessarily so, it is well not to start with the assumption that it is so.

3. DISTINGUISH BETWEEN THE APPEARANCE AND THE REALITY.

Appearances can be deceiving. Try not to be deceived by them. Always remain open to the possibility that what appears to be true may not be. The student who avoids the company of others, who does not speak when you pass him on the campus, appears to be a snob who feels he is too good to associate with other students. Perhaps he is a snob—but perhaps he is just shy and introverted. On the other hand, the "pal" who is quite devoted to you, accompanies you on every evening out, and is extremely solicitous of your welfare, certainly appears to be a close friend to you. Perhaps he is —but perhaps he really likes your *car* and the free transportation it represents. Similarly, draft-card burning may seem to be the most responsible way to protest the present selective service system. Perhaps it is the most responsible way—but perhaps not. Don't be satisfied with appearances. Ask if what seems to be so is really so.

4. DISTINGUISH BETWEEN THE PERSON AND HIS IDEA.

A truly wonderful person may have a ridiculous idea. And a despicable person may have an excellent idea. The economics professor you most admire as a person and a teacher may have an absurd political philosophy. The always engaging, entertaining and eloquent psychology professor, whose courses students flock to take, may have an irrational prejudice against religion. And your minister, priest, or rabbi, though an inspiringly spiritual man, humble, wise, and much loved by his congregation, may have an equally irrational prejudice against psychology. On the other hand, the low-marking, non-curving, somewhat caustic English professor, the bane of the student body, may occasionally offer you a profound observation about life. You can guard against the normal human tendency to accept the ideas of those you like and to dismiss the ideas of those you dislike by making the distinction between the man and his idea, by taking special care to question the arguments of those you like, or those writers whose general viewpoint you share, and by going out of your way to be objective in considering the arguments of those you do not like, or those writers whose general viewpoint you do not share. "One must look to where the banners go," observed Edmond and Jules de Goncourt, "and not to those who carry them."

5. DISTINGUISH BETWEEN WHY A PERSON THINKS AS HE DOES AND WHETHER WHAT HE THINKS IS CORRECT.

It has been fashionable for a number of years for critics to "psychoanalyze" characters in literature and even speculate about what forces in authors' lives influenced them to create certain characters and choose certain themes. It would be incautious to suggest that such studies have no place as intellectual pursuits. Obviously they do. It is proper and fruitful, for example, to consider why a character in fiction acts as he does, or to consider why our opponent in argument holds a different view from ours. In both these cases, our purpose in speculating about the "why" of his actions or ideas is to achieve a better understanding of the person. But this same approach is of little value when we are evaluating a person's *idea*. The belief that we may dismiss a person's idea once we have explained why he holds it is a fallacy, and a very misleading one. Remember that a man may hit upon a profound idea for the silliest of reasons, and avoid thinking that your comments about his motivations validate or invalidate his idea.

6. DISTINGUISH BETWEEN WHAT IS SAID AND THE WAY IT IS SAID.

The possibility of error is not only an affliction of the inarticulate. A person may have a rare gift for choosing just the right words for his idea. He may have a moving style that commands his reader's attention and appeals to his frame of reference. He may have all these gifts and yet on occasion present an unsound argument. Still that argument may be convincing. The only way we can guard against being deceived by style is to distinguish between the thought and the expression. Consider this passage:

> . . . It is a great and dangerous error to suppose that all people are equally entitled to liberty. It is a reward to be earned, not a blessing to be gratuitously lavished on all alike;—a reward reserved for the intelligent, the patriotic, the virtuous and deserving;—and not a boon to be bestowed on a people too ignorant, degraded and vicious, to be capable either of appreciating or of enjoying it.[4]

Well said. And yet, most of us would agree, fallacious. The problem is that a foolish, shallow, or utterly false idea can elicit a favorable response from us if it is expressed well. And a sound idea can elicit an unfavorable response if it is expressed poorly. Therefore, in evaluating ideas, we do well to remember Augustine's observation, "Our concern with a man is not with what eloquence he teaches, but with what evidence."

7. DISTINGUISH BETWEEN WHAT IS SAID AND WHAT IS IMPLIED.

It is often the implication rather than the explicit statement that you will wish to question. Consider this situation. The flower-bed in front of your dormitory has been trampled. Your dormitory supervisor calls a meeting of everyone living in your dorm. He makes this statement:

[4] John C. Calhoun, "Disquisition on Government," first published in 1954. Reprinted in E. L. McKitrick, ed., *Slavery Defended; the Views of the Old South* (Englewood Cliffs, N.J.: Prentice-Hall, Inc., 1963), p. 53.

The college paid a good deal of money for those flowers. And now some boor who never was brought up to appreciate beauty nor to respect the property of others has destroyed them. I don't know who did it. But I'll tell you this. Unless the offender steps forward now, the TV room in this dorm will be closed for a month as a punishment for this vandalism.

The statement bothers you. You wish to answer the supervisor and tell him why you are bothered. But if you consider just what he said and miss what he implied, you will surely miss the main thing that bothers you—the unstated idea that the person responsible was necessarily someone from your dorm. If you realized that your objection was more to what he implied than to what he said, you would answer, "You say that the offender must step forward or else we all will be punished. The implication is that one of us who live in this dorm must have trampled the flowers. But there are two other dorms within fifty yards of the flower-bed. And four hundred students live in them. Any one of them could easily have done it, just to cause trouble for us. Is it fair to punish us if you're not sure we're to blame?" Remember that the idea that is left unsaid is often the very idea that requires careful examination.

8. DISTINGUISH BETWEEN WHAT IS SAID AND WHAT YOU WISH WERE SAID.

The students of a certain college object to the college policy on "cutting" classes, and they stage a demonstration to show their feelings. The next day in one class a student asks the professor what he thinks of the previous night's demonstration. The professor answers as follows:

> I really can't give any opinion about the reasonableness of the students' position. I wasn't at the rally, so I didn't hear the speeches. I will say, though, that I would favor such a demonstration only when students have exhausted all other means of expressing their views to faculty and administration.

One of the students in class jots down a reminder to mention Professor Jackson's statement at that night's rally. That night at the rally the student stands on an orange crate and says, "Today in class we asked Professor Jackson what he thought of our demonstration. He said he's on our side."

That student heard *what he wanted to hear* instead of what the professor was saying. It is a common mistake. Whenever we hear a speech or read an article, there is a natural tendency for us to confuse what is said with what we wish were said. This is particularly so when what is said sharply opposes our own position. It seems that some sort of defense mechanism is responsible for the illusion. Or perhaps it is intellectual sloth, the subconscious reluctance to acknowledge the existence of an opposing idea and the challenge it poses for us.

Whatever the cause, it is important to guard against this reaction. Whenever you listen to or read the words of others, be careful to understand what they really say, regardless of what you want them to say.

9. DISTINGUISH BETWEEN THE RECOGNIZED SIDE OF A TRUTH AND THE NEGLECTED SIDE.

G. K. Chesterton once suggested that "a thinking man should always attack the strongest thing in his own time. For the strongest thing is always too strong." Everyone needs to remind himself from time to time of the side of a truth thinkers in his day tend to overlook. No time in history has been characterized by complete balance of outlook on every issue. On most issues, especially the most controversial, there is usually an emphasis on one side of the truth, frequently the side that the previous age neglected. Therefore, the careful thinker never yields completely to the siren-song of his day. He constantly reminds himself and others of the neglected side.

The Place of Reasoning in Writing

The quality of our reasoning governs the quality of our writing more directly than any other single element of rhetoric. No vividness of detail, no felicity of expression, no strength of feeling can compensate for flawed reasoning. This fact, of course, does not mean that vividness of detail or felicity of expression are unimportant. They are important, as are all the other elements of rhetoric. Nor does it mean that reasoning should in any way displace feeling. (Rather, it should help us distinguish between feelings of greater and those of lesser worth.) It means that before we begin writing about an issue, it is important to think about it carefully—to accumulate whatever evidence we can, to identify possible impediments to reasoning and important distinctions to be made, and to be conscious of our own limitations. Not every one of the problems raised in this essay will occur in every writing situation; some will occur very frequently, others only occasionally. Until we get used to them and learn to ask the related questions almost automatically, applying this material can seem a little mechanical. We must ask many more questions than are relevant to the issue. And the more we have tended to rely on intuition or "common sense," the more difficult it is to work slowly and purposefully and not leap to conclusions. Furthermore, precisely at those moments when we are least inclined to reason carefully, when we are tempted to say, "Here is the answer; I know it; I'm positive," we need most to slow down and examine the idea carefully.

When we have established a tentative position, a main idea, it is helpful to develop a rough plan of how we intend to organize and present our thoughts. But it is well to remember that neither the preliminary thinking nor the rough plan should preclude changes in our thinking as we write. Some of our best reasoning may occur *during* the writing process. The act of writing can be an act of discovery. The physical motions of writing or typing a series of sentences can trigger questions about our preliminary reasoning; and if we acknowledge those questions and pause to consider them, we can often discover contradictions in our thinking that we were unaware of, superficialities or gaps in our understanding of certain aspects of the issue, deficiencies in our reasoning.

Accordingly, we should regard early drafts of any piece of our writing as means not only of expressing our reasoning, but also of extending it, modifying it, even (if the situation demands) reversing it.

2

Persuasion

As the previous essay pointed out, the foundation of good writing is sound reasoning. The concern of this essay is with a closely related matter, the task of presenting our ideas effectively to others. That task is called persuasion. Persuasion is not the purpose of every piece of writing,[1] but in much of the most important writing we do, it is not only a purpose, but the dominant one. Writing for the purpose of persuasion does not exclude other considerations of rhetoric. All the other elements of rhetoric—the quality of the reasoning and matters of substance, organization, and style—remain important considerations. Persuasion is a matter that goes beyond these. For even a composition that displays the writer's mastery of these can be quite *un*persuasive. The concern of this essay is with those matters that enhance or destroy the effectiveness of our writing.

The context of all persuasive writing[2] is argument. The issue is always, to some extent, controversial. Our readers will therefore either agree with us already, be open to suggestion, or disagree with us. Each group will feel strongly about their position. *Those*

---

[1] For a discussion of the range of purposes in writing, see "Purpose in Writing" in "Other Elements of Rhetoric."

[2] Although throughout this essay persuasion is discussed in the context of writing, what is said here applies to speaking as well. Thus, references to "the writer" or "the reader" may also be understood as "the speaker" or "the listener."

24

who agree with us are not of concern in this essay. They will be relatively uncritical of our presentation since it supports their own position. But the other groups will be very critical, and therefore difficult to persuade. Those who are neutral are open to suggestion, but if they are intelligent and educated—as every sensible writer assumes his readers are—they will be willing to accept what we say only if it is reasonable to them. Those who disagree with us are most difficult to write for because they have strong beliefs, sometimes developed through hours of study and reflection.

It would be naive to expect those who have strong convictions to set them aside after reading an essay explaining an opposite viewpoint. Whether the argument is pursued in the pages of a scholarly journal or in a college newspaper, no mature writer expects those who disagree with him to read his position and immediately concede that he is right and they have been wrong. Therefore the term "persuasion," as it is used in this essay, does *not* mean convincing others of the correctness of one's position. Rather it means *presenting one's view to best advantage, disposing those who are neutral or opposed to reflect on his view and reconsider their own in light of it.*

Considering the Reader

The first problem that persuasive writing poses for the apprentice writer is thinking of someone other than himself. He must think of his reader. And a reader is limited to his own frame of reference, his own experiences, observations, and thought patterns. When he encounters unsupported assertions, he depends on that frame of reference; he literally has nothing else by which to measure the assertions. There is, of course, a chance that the reader's frame of reference will *approximate* the writer's, but the fact that each person's experiences, like his fingerprints, are unique makes even that chance rather slight.

Therefore, the writer who merely tells the reader what he thinks not only bores the reader, but runs the unnecessary risk of having his idea misunderstood. The wise writer devotes the greater part of his writing to presenting evidence—that is, he *shows* the reader the validity of his assertion, provides not only the conclusion he has reached, but the experiences and observations, the sensory impressions, the steps in reasoning that have led him to that conclusion.

Similarly, the writer who permits no compromise between bluntness and tact frequently jeopardizes his chances of persuading his reader. Granted that strong feelings about an issue tempt one to write a "blast" against some "hypocrisy;" granted even that there is a great sense of satisfaction and achievement in yielding to that temptation. Still, such an approach, however effective it may be with those who share the writer's view, is completely ineffective with those who do not, and never really effective with neutral readers. Consider this example:

> Many students say they are treated like children at home, so they come to college to be treated like adults. Then they wear their hair over their ears, their jeans skintight and cut off at the knee, and sport lice-infested beards, and sandals. In short, they reek with non-conformist conformity.

To readers who share this writer's attitude toward those he is criticizing the passage is uproariously funny and seems incisively logical. But it is not so to the campus non-conformists. They feel the writer is being unfair, sees only what he wants to see, and rather deviously weaves his insults about their appearance into a contrived context—the suggestion that they are childish.

Such acid comment, to be sure, occurs as well in the writing of professionals, as the following example reveals:

> . . . We do not really need, it seems to me, another compendium such as *The People Look at Television* by Gary Steiner. Rather, the scholars should look at Gary Steiner to learn how he compiled 400 pages of graphs, charts, and sociological prattle without really saying anything. The book is almost unreadable and is boring.[3]

Now to an English instructor the word play on the title of the book and reference to the jargon of sociology are amusing. But to Gary Steiner the personal reference would be offensive, and to sociologists the term "sociological prattle" would seem uncalled-for. The passage is excusable only because the writer knew his audience and therefore knew that their reaction would be amusement.

Interestingly, the apprentice writer's awareness of the importance

---

[3] John H. Lerch, "Communications Study: An Illusion of Purpose?" *College Composition and Communication*, October, 1964, p. 152.

of considering his reader sometimes creates another problem. The moment he realizes that the effectiveness of his work depends not only on force, but more importantly on persuasion, he tends to forget that the main purpose of any writing, persuasive included, is *to convey his ideas honestly.* He is prone to weak, tepid writing, which is surely a more serious fault. And its consequences are grave. "If a writer is so cautious that he never writes anything that cannot be criticized," Thomas Merton warns, "he will never write anything that can be read. If you want to help other people, you have got to make up your mind to write things that some men will condemn." [4] The effective writer strives to gain both force and persuasiveness by constantly asking himself, "Where in this piece of writing must force yield to tact and where tact to force?" Sometimes the choice is not easy, as the following passage illustrates (emphasis mine):

> Two members of the present Court, Justices Black and Douglas, seem to take a fairly absolutist position with regard to freedom of speech. An occasional philosophical writer, such as Alexander Meiklejohn, reads the First Amendment as "an absolute, unqualified prohibition." But even Meiklejohn is not to be taken quite so literally as he seems to take the First Amendment, for he is quick to recognize the legitimacy of forbidding libelous and slanderous words, or words inciting men to crime, or sedition and treason expressed in speech and writing. *He satisfies his own instinct for consistency* by explaining that the First Amendment does not forbid the abridging of speech, but only the abridging of the freedom of speech. Thus Meiklejohn *manages to eat his cake and have it at the same time, a miracle beyond the capacity of most ordinary mortals who are deficient in the talent for sentence-squeezing.*
> At the other extreme, of course, are the people who reject, more or less, the whole concept of free speech. Thus a young scholar recently wrote a book to argue that the Court should construe the First Amendment, not to safeguard freedom primarily, but to promote morality and virtue. If, as he argues, the right to speak extends only to the speaking of the right things, I shall have to suspend any serious judgment concerning the merits of his thesis *until he gets around to explaining what is right and what is wrong.* Since this problem was wrestled with by such philosophical and moral luminaries as Isaiah and Jeremiah, Plato and Aristotle, St. Augustine and St. Thomas, Gautama Buddha, Confucius, and Bertrand Russell, *I await the word of this latter-day apostle of virtue and justice with considerable interest.* It may well turn out that there is a lot

[4] *Seeds of Contemplation* (New York: Dell Publishing Company, 1949), p. 65.

of truth in the observation that "the books are balanced in heaven, not here." [5]

This writer's use of sarcasm is a risk, I assume a calculated one. His audience's reaction was not at all so predictable as Lerch's. For he wrote the book for an intellectual audience that might well share the views of Meiklejohn and the "young scholar." Those readers who do share their views will certainly react unfavorably to the sarcasm. Apparently the writer felt that the situation demanded complete frankness, despite the risk that his words might work against persuasion. Obviously, if he could have made his point as forcefully without sarcasm, the risk would have been lessened.

The problem of being persuasive without losing force exists not only for the writer. It exists as well for the courtroom lawyer. He must constantly be aware of the effect of his words upon the jury as well as upon the witness. In his classic book on courtroom practice, *The Art of Cross-Examination*, Francis L. Wellman explains the importance of this awareness:

If the cross-examiner allows the witness to suspect, from his manner toward him at the start, that he distrusts his integrity, he will straighten himself in the witness chair and mentally defy him at once. If, on the other hand, the counsel's manner is courteous and conciliatory, the witness will soon lose the fear all witnesses have of the cross-examiner, and can almost imperceptibly be induced to enter into a discussion of his testimony in a fair minded spirit, which, if the cross-examiner is clever, will soon disclose the weak points in the testimony. The sympathies of the jury are invariably on the side of the witness, and they are quick to resent any discourtesy toward him. They are willing to admit his *mistakes*, if you can make them apparent, but are slow to believe him *guilty of perjury*. Alas, how often this is lost sight of in our daily court experiences! One is constantly brought face to face with lawyers who act as if they thought that every one who testifies against their side of the case is committing wilful perjury. No wonder they accomplish so little with their *cross*-examination! By their shouting, browbeating style they often confuse the wits of the witness, it is true; but they fail to discredit him with the jury. On the contrary, they elicit sympathy for the witness they are attacking, and little realize that their "vigorous cross-examination," at the end of which they sit down with evident self-satisfaction, has only served to close effectually the mind of at least one fair minded juryman against their side of the case, and as likely as not it has brought to light some important

[5] David Fellman, *The Limits of Freedom* (New Brunswick, New Jersey: Rutgers University Press, 1959), pp. 55-56. Used with permission.

fact favorable to the other side which had been overlooked in the examination-in-chief.[6]

The reader of an article or book, of course, cannot in the strict sense be regarded as a jury. But he does indeed render judgment on what he reads, and the good writer, like the good cross-examiner, is attentive to the way his words influence that judgment.

Perhaps the most ludicrous mistake that the writer can make in this regard is to pretend he knows more than he does, to masquerade his inadequate knowledge of the facts of an issue in bravado. If his readers cannot expose him, they seldom are deceived by the pretense. And if they can expose him—that is, if they know exactly in what way he is wrong—he is seen as an utter fool, very similar to the "inexperienced young attorney" in the following example:

An inexperienced young attorney was defending his client on a charge of murder, claiming that the death was the result of suicide and not homicide. An elderly German physician had made the autopsy and had testified that after a very careful examination of the course of the bullet as it entered and passed through the body, he was satisfied that it could not possibly have been self-inflicted. The witness offered diagrams illustrating his point, and if his opinion should be accepted by the jury, there could no longer be any question of suicide.

The young attorney started his cross-examination by addressing the witness in a rather flippant and disrespectful manner which, naturally, irritated the witness, somewhat along these lines:

Attorney: "Dr. _____, you seem very certain about your finding in this case. You do not give it as your opinion that the wound in this case could not have been self-inflicted, but you state it as a matter of fact—swear to it as a matter of fact. Now I'd like to ask you—by any chance is this the first autopsy you have ever made? I don't find your name anywhere in our local Medical Directory."

Doctor (sitting back in his seat and answering very quietly, holding up one of his hands and apparently counting his fingers). "No, I can say that I have made a previous autopsy."

Attorney (apparently encouraged by his answer). "Well, could you honestly say that you have made two autopsies, not counting this one?"

Doctor (again hesitating, and again counting his open fingers, apparently reminiscing). "Yes, I think I can truthfully say I have made two prior autopsies."

Attorney (still more encouraged). "Well, can you go so far as to say that you have made five autopsies?"

Doctor (this time examining his outstretched hand very deliberately and apparently touching the tip of each finger as he counted up his cases before making a reply, and then looking up pleasantly at the attorney). "Yes—yes, I think I can say that I have made as many as five autopsies."

Attorney (exultant and with a scornful smile, walking toward the witness). "Well, sir, why beat about the bush? Let's put it this way. Can you say you have made ten thousand previous autopsies?"

Doctor (with a broad, rather amused smile on his face, but still in a low tone). "Well, I think I can truthfully say I probably have. *You see I was Coroner for forty years in the City of Berlin before I came to this country!!!*" [7]

The point? It is dangerous for a speaker or writer to be presumptuous about his audience. The reader, of course, is not able to humble the writer as the doctor did the young attorney—openly and dramatically, with an audience. He can only do so in his own mind. But the mere thought of countless readers doing even that should be sufficient to deter a writer from empty demonstrations of knowledge or expertise.

Some Principles of Persuasion

We make our writing persuasive by combining skillful application of other rules of rhetoric with observance of the following basic principles of persuasion. The reference to the reader in each case is to one who holds the opposing view, rather than a neutral view. It is easier to be cautious with an audience, even a neutral audience, if we approach them as if they opposed our view.

1. ADMIT THAT YOUR READER IS SINCERE IN HIS BELIEF. UNDERSTAND AND RESPECT HIM.

When we are speaking to another person, it is easy enough for us to tell whether or not he respects us. If he regards us as dolts or fools or hypocrites, no matter how much he attempts to hide his

[7] Wellman, *The Art of Cross-Examination*, pp. 96-97.

feelings, they will be revealed, and usually quite clearly, in his tone of voice, his facial expressions, his choice of phrasing. In writing we cannot hear his tone of voice or see his facial expressions, but we do see his choice of phrasing. And this is usually a sufficient measure of his attitude toward us for us to understand and react to. What is our reaction in such a case? Usually resentment and some degree of hostility toward him and toward what he is saying, *especially if what he is saying challenges our own position.* The point to remember is that YOUR READER WILL REACT PRECISELY THIS WAY UNLESS YOU UNDERSTAND AND RESPECT HIM.

Understanding another can only be achieved by asking why he might think as he does. Is he against helping the poor? Perhaps at one time he gave freely to the poor of his time and money. Perhaps he did so because he was very idealistic, and it was the shattering of this very idealism by a few contacts with unappreciative, lazy poor people that turned him against helping the poor. You have no way of telling if that actually happened. Perhaps it didn't. Perhaps he is against helping the poor because he is selfish and hard and cold. If you think he is selfish and hard and cold, do not write to persuade him, for if you do try you will certainly be ineffective. *Your disrespect is sure to show through your words.* Write for another reader, one you can respect, whose sincerity you may think is misplaced but which you nevertheless can acknowledge (such as the formerly idealistic person I mentioned above).

As pointed out in the previous essay, we must distinguish between the person and his idea. To the person we owe the benefit of the doubt, simply because he is a person and a person's mind is too complex and mysterious for us to know. He may hold his position because he was never taught any differently and never learned to evaluate what he was taught, or because he was intimately involved with the matter himself. On the subject of poverty he may hold his view because he himself grew up in a poor family, one perhaps in which the poverty was due to his parents' sloth rather than to any real misfortune. Or because he was never involved with the matter, he has based his decision only on what he has read, and has read some persuasive but fallacious books and articles.

When you fail to take this broad-minded, charitable approach, when you persist in the attitude that your opponent differs with you because he is willfully dishonest, you court failure in persuasion, as the following writers did:

a) A student was writing about the problems of his campus for an audience of his college administrators. He concluded his composition with this sentence:

> By being honest with each other and trying to improve the situation, administrators could greatly reduce these problems.

The statement is unnecessarily offensive to the readers. The hostility is thinly veiled, because though the writer doesn't explicitly accuse them of dishonesty, he clearly implies this accusation. Why would he suggest that they be honest unless he believes they are at present dishonest?

b) Another student was writing in his campus newspaper about a particular campus problem, the cancelling of all student parties and activities during the week preceding final examinations. He concluded his composition as follows:

> It's about time the administration woke up to the fact that the students on this campus are human. Right now the tension on the campus is extremely high due to approaching finals. The release of this tension will help the students study for finals—believe it or not!

Suggesting that the administration wake up implies that they are asleep. And to be asleep to so fundamental a fact as that students are human is to be rather stupid. "Believe it or not" in this context implies that they are unable or unwilling to recognize one of the most elementary facts of psychology.

c) A third student was writing a composition to an audience of students who complain about instructors' harshness in dealing with students who don't know their work. His point was that instructors often have a reason to be harsh. He included this sentence in his paper:

> Have you ever been in an algebra class where a student has done a problem wrong? Of course you have; everyone makes mistakes, even you.

The "even you" adds nothing to his idea. All it does is insult the readers and make them defensive, an extravagance the writer who wishes to be persuasive can ill afford.

2. UNDERSTAND AND APPRECIATE YOUR READER'S POSITION.
YOU MUST KNOW WHERE HE STANDS BEFORE YOU CAN
HOPE TO REACH HIM.

The writer who does not trouble to understand and appreciate his reader's position on the matter in question, who merely fires his composition in the general direction of the argument, gets at best the effect of a shotgun blast—covering a wide area, but giving no concentration. But the writer who, before writing, spends some time examining his reader's position and appraising it correctly, gets the effect of a rifle shot—delivering his argument directly to the target.

It is not easy to understand and appreciate an opponent's position. As Lord Halifax said, "Nothing has an uglier look to us than reason, when it is not of our side." But however difficult understanding and appreciation are to achieve, they are essential in persuasion.

Consider, for example, the case of a student who feels strongly that college students should not be allowed to drink beer and liquor on the campus. He picks up a copy of his college newspaper one day and sees an editorial that argues for a lifting of the ban on alcohol on campus. The editor reasons that (1) the students at present have to drive five miles to the nearest bar and frequently endanger their lives by recklessly speeding to return before curfew, (2) several other area colleges recently lifted their bans on campus drinking, and (3) the vast majority of the students are over 18 and therefore could be expected to handle the privilege of on-campus drinking responsibly. The editor concludes with an appeal to the college administration to reconsider their ban on drinking on campus.

The student puts down the paper, walks to his desk, and begins typing a letter to the editor, muttering in anger. After several minutes of typing he sits back and reads his first paragraphs, nodding in agreement with himself. He reads:

Editor of the *Campus Bugle*:

I just finished reading your editorial in this week's paper. It didn't fool me a bit. I see through your "pitch." But perhaps there are a few gullible students on this campus who will miss the point. So

I'll explain it for their sake. You want a campus souse-house—no, it's worse than that—you want every room on campus to be a souse-house. You want students lying all over campus, fried to oblivion. You want a drunken orgy in every room. And you're not going to be satisfied until you succeed in dragging the rest of us down to your level.

He smiles, and begins typing again. But we've read enough. He's just ruined what could have been an effective answer. He violated the first principle of persuasion, of course. His disrespect of the editor (and by implication anyone who agrees with the editor) comes through only too clearly. But more to the point here, he has violated the second principle of persuasion. The editor had a rationale for his position. But the student was too busy disagreeing to study it and learn its strengths and weaknesses. He could only think of refuting it, and he was unconcerned whether or not he was accurately interpreting it. One thing is certain—his refusal to deal fairly with the editorial and the editor will not go unnoticed by the editor or by the students who read his letter. Unpersuasive? Yes. So much so that he may drive some neutral readers to support the editor's view, rather than reject it.

If his reaction had not been so glandular, he might have studied the editor's arguments carefully enough to see that the editor has one very good point, number 1. The five-mile drive is inconvenient and the return trip is probably dangerous. His second point is not good. It's really little more than the old "band-wagon," propaganda technique, though he may have used it innocently—what others are doing may not be the best thing to do, and what is best for one campus is not necessarily best for another. His third point, considered by itself, may be valid. Perhaps the majority of the students could handle on-campus drinking responsibly. But considered together with his first point it raises the question, "If these students would drink responsibly, why is it they can't drive home from a bar responsibly?"

Perhaps, too, if the letter writer had been less quick to judge he would have judged better. Perhaps he would have thought to suggest to the editor that having a drink away from campus is more relaxing, that work and play may be done better in separate places. He might not have convinced the editor, but he might have made him think a little more about the subject. And he probably would have impressed a few other students.

3. BEGIN FROM A POSITION YOU HAVE IN COMMON WITH THE
READER, FROM A POINT OF AGREEMENT RATHER THAN
DISAGREEMENT.

Beginning from a position of agreement with your reader is not
an arbitrary requirement or a matter of courtesy or "good form." *It
is a simple matter of psychology.* Any sound structure demands a
firm foundation, and nowhere is this more valid than in human
communications, especially in areas of disagreement where the
tendency to hostility is strong.

If you begin by saying—in effect if not directly—"look here, you
are wrong, and I'm going to show you," you push your reader to a
defensive if not outright hostile reaction. He is likely to read the
rest of your paper thinking not of what you are saying, but of ways
to refute it, concerned with measuring not the validity of your
arguments, but only their invalidity. And if he is unreasonable and
unbalanced in his reading, the fault will be more yours than his.

In the persuasive composition, regardless of the issue or the
words used, the beginning says in effect—though never directly—
"You and I are both interested in this subject, we both regard it as
a serious and important one, and though our positions differ on
many points, by communicating with each other we can further
develop our positions and move a little closer toward the elusive
truth that is our common goal." I am referring here to *the attitude*
displayed in the beginning, indeed throughout, the composition. It
is not something that can be *stated* in the beginning, or in any
other place in the composition. It is virtually impossible to state
without the ring of insincerity or at least the effect of embarrass-
ment for writer and reader alike. Yet it must be present.

It is always difficult to find any points of agreement with someone whose views you strongly disagree with. This was the case with
the student who wrote his composition supporting the view that
students who fail out of his college should be allowed to apply for
readmission. His readers were administrators who had expressed
the view that they should not. He began as follows:

> I think students who fail out of this college should be allowed to
> apply for readmission because every student deserves a second

chance. You have said that most readmits lack seriousness of purpose. But . . . .

This student was probably quite sure that he and his readers could agree on nothing. So he began with a head-on collision that wrecked his chances to be persuasive. The readers' reaction, conscious or unconscious, undoubtedly was: "This student sees only his own biased position. He doesn't understand the complexity of the problem, doesn't consider the welfare of the total student body, apparently doesn't appreciate that a college education is not a right at all, but a privilege." Their reaction would be mistaken. The student may have been fully aware of all these considerations. But he failed to show his readers that he was. How much better an impression he would have made if he had begun like this:

No one benefits—neither teachers nor other students—from the presence on campus of students for whom college means merely fun, or a rest, or a chance to make social contacts. Such students take up precious time and space, and usually serve only to distract more serious students. They fail in most cases to realize that a college education is a privilege that they must continue to earn, not an inviolable right. I agree that this college has its share of such students.

The "but" would still appear. The student would still argue his point, but only after he had impressed his readers with the scope of his understanding of the issue and with his desire to be reasonable.

4. TAKE A POSITIVE APPROACH. WHENEVER POSSIBLE, BUILD YOUR CASE INSTEAD OF TEARING DOWN YOUR OPPONENT'S.

There will always be times, even with the most controversial of issues, when being persuasive is extremely difficult, when you will have to violate this rule in part. You will find it necessary to point out an error in your opponent's reasoning or to submit one or two of his points to direct analysis. But remember that thinking about his points and deciding how you can best counter them does not necessarily mean that you must present a direct refutation of them.

But even though you feel on occasion that there is no effective alternative to such direct refutation, you should remember that this negative approach—tearing down his case—always involves greater risk than simply building your own. And the risk is making him defensive. Having an idea you have formed with a great deal of effort demolished is not unlike losing an arm or a leg. The idea is a part of you, and having it taken away is always painful.

Consider, for example, this writing situation. Someone writes an article attacking anti-gun legislation. Two responses are printed in the following issue of the magazine. In summary the article and responses read as follows:

ARTICLE	RESPONSE TO ARTICLE
Anti-gun legislation (a) penalizes the law-abiding more than the lawless, (b) denies citizens the most effective means of protecting self and property at a time when assaults on both are commonplace, (c) violates the U.S. Constitution.	1. Anti-gun legislation does not penalize the law-abiding more than the lawless. It does not deny citizens the most effective means of protection. It does not really violate the U.S. Constitution. 2. Anti-gun legislation discourages crime by making the mere possession of a gun an offense of some gravity. It stresses the role of the police, rather than the individual, in law-enforcement. It follows the spirit, if not the letter, of the U.S. Constitution.

Both responses disagree with the article on each of the three points it raised. But the first merely tears down the article's position; the second builds another position. In effect, the first says to the article-writer, "You are wrong, you are wrong, you are wrong"; the second says, "Here is another view." Whenever you can avoid direct refutation—that is, whenever you can as effectively present and support your own views without direct reference to your reader's opposing views—do so.

5. IN DISCUSSING YOUR POSITION ON THE SHARPEST POINTS OF CONTENTION, UNDERSTATE YOUR ARGUMENT.

The sharpest points of disagreement between you and your reader should always be approached most carefully. These points represent the greatest obstacle to persuasion. If you overstate your position, you are bound to reinforce your reader's conviction about his position rather than dispose him to question his conviction. The student who wrote the following passage made this blunder:

Most colleges have a "cut system"—that is, they permit a student a few unexcused absences from class without penalty. This college permits no unexcused absences. Its system is harsh and uncompromising, and may well cause students to develop inferiority complexes.

The reader, who in this case supports the college's "no-cut" system, is here not only reinforced in his position by the "inferiority complex" *overstatement*, but is provided with an excellent opportunity for damaging rebuttal, which he would handle as follows:

That this college's "no-cut" system is demanding, I grant. But the suggestion that it causes students to "develop inferiority complexes" strains credibility. However, even if it were established that it does in fact cause such complexes, would we not be driven to the conclusion that students in such psychologically fragile condition need not fewer but *more* restrictions to prevent their breakdown?

The student who wrote the following passage made a similar mistake.

If others treat us with respect and admiration we will become more respectable and admirable.

He overstated the effect. The respect and admiration of others may encourage us to be respectable and admirable, but it will certainly not automatically make us so. The costliness of the mistake is measured by the fact that the reader, who would have tended to agree with understatement, is likely to reject the whole idea because of the writer's careless use of force.

Consider the following two passages, particularly the italicized words. The first is the forceful statement the writer was tempted to make. The second is the statement he actually made. It is an *understatement*. Note that it does not compromise the writer's position, but it does present the idea more effectively to a reader who would be inclined to disagree.

1. If college students are not given *opportunities* to exercise responsibility and make their own choices while they are in college, they will have to adjust *all at once* when they leave college. And such adjustment will be *extremely difficult*.
2. If college students are not given *some opportunities* to exercise responsibility and make their own choices while they are in college, they will have to adjust rather quickly when they leave college. And such adjustment will *usually* be *more difficult*.

6. CONCEDE WHERE YOUR OPPONENT HAS A POINT, AND DO SO GRACIOUSLY, GENEROUSLY, AND SINCERELY.

The natural tendency in all of us to value our own position too highly makes it difficult for us to admit the validity of our opponent's position. Overcoming this tendency can be accomplished only by remembering that in most controversial issues *no one side possesses the total truth.* The writer who can approach a controversial issue with this thought is more likely to approach the total truth, and to attract reasonable readers to his position.

Total commitment to the truth obliges us, moreover, to concede not grudgingly, but gladly and without hesitation. This does not mean placing a single short sentence at the beginning of the composition that says "Everyone is right in some degree; I suppose you are too," and then launching into your own position. It means a specific and, if space permits, a detailed explanation of where, how, and why he is correct.

Let's say, for example, that the issue is whether a comprehensive sex education program from kindergarten through twelfth grade should be initiated in your home town. Your argument is that it should be. You reason that since a person's whole life is affected by the quality of his understanding of sex, it is too important a subject to be learned in the street; and that, since many parents neglect their responsibility to teach their children at home, the school must offer such a program. Your readers are opposed to the program because they feel that the school classroom permits neither the direction of instruction to the individual child at his level of understanding nor the moral-religious context they believe sex education should have. Any reasonable person would admit that the readers' points are well taken. Therefore, you should concede that it is difficult to identify those students whose level of maturity is significantly below the rest of the class, and that the presentation of material well beyond their grasp could be disturbing to them. Further, you should concede that, ideally, the home is the best place for the young to learn about sex, that the school cannot provide the moral-religious context that many parents consider essential. These concessions will not undermine your position. You will still be able to argue that the program is necessary, though you will probably have to qualify your endorsement, acknowledging that the details of the program must be worked out in light of your concessions and that teachers should be selected with great care. The concessions will actually have enhanced your argument, for they demonstrate your grasp of the larger dimensions of the question.

Remember that the reader will give you as much as you give him, usually no less and no more. Only if you are open and honest in your concessions can you expect him to be in his.

7. DON'T IGNORE ANY RELEVANT FACTS, EVEN UNPLEASANT ONES.

In studying an issue, we sometimes uncover facts that support our opponent's position rather than our own. The temptation is strong to ignore them, especially if our opponent has apparently not discovered them. Using them, it would seem, could only weaken our position.

However, the purpose of argument is not to defeat one's opponent, but through the exchange of views to discover the truth in all its complexity. When that happens, everyone wins. When any part of the truth is hidden, no one wins, even though it may appear that someone does. By presenting all the facts, even those that force you to modify your position, you impress your reader with your objectivity and honesty and invite him to show his.

Consider the following situation. You believe that the present federally-directed anti-poverty program is more beneficial to the poor than the proposed state-directed program would be. You are researching the subject further, preparing to write an article supporting your position for an audience of those who disagree with you. In researching the question you discover a not widely publicized report documenting serious inefficiency and waste in the present federal program. Moreover, it seems clear that these inefficiencies would be less likely to occur in the proposed program. You realize that your reader probably has not seen this report and that it would be damaging to your original position to mention it in your article. What should you do? If you have good reason to conclude that the report is not really relevant to the issue, it would be foolish to mention it. However, if you were convinced that it was relevant—in other words, if it caused you to modify your original position—honesty would require you to mention it and deal with the questions it raised.

8. DON'T TRY TO OVERWHELM YOUR READER. LIMIT YOUR
ARGUMENTS TO THOSE YOU FEEL ARE MOST IMPORTANT
SO THAT THE READER DOESN'T GET THE IMPRESSION YOU
ARE FORCING HIM.

The short paper (any paper of less than 10,000 words must in controversial matters be considered short) cannot be definitive. No serious writer would attempt to convey the impression that it is. Of necessity it contains *selected* evidence. On the surface it would seem that this would give more reason to fill the paper to overflowing with evidence for one's position, to make it as nearly definitive as possible. But on consideration it is clear that the reader's impression must be considered too. What is the impression of a reader who reads a composition or article which he knows cannot possibly be definitive, but which devotes all or nearly all its space to arguing for one side of an issue, piling detail on detail, example on example, without ever even implying that there is another side to the issue? There is no question that he will regard it as *one-sided* and *unbalanced*! The way to avoid such an unfavorable reader reaction is to present only those arguments and that evidence which you feel are most relevant, most persuasive to him.

There is one other related point. Even when a writer succeeds in avoiding an unbalanced argument, he sometimes gets so taken up with his presentation that he pushes the reader, usually by concluding his paper like this:

I think *I have proven* in this paper that there is no alternative to the one suggested by Professor Jones.

or

The evidence I have presented *seems irrefutable*. There *can be no question* that the proposal is harmful.

or

The *reasonable person* will not hesitate to endorse this view.

If the writer thinks he has "proven" anything in a short paper, he is deceiving himself. His evidence may "seem irrefutable" to him and he may see "no question," but he should remember that it is wiser to permit the reader to make his own judgment. And no reader enjoys feeling that he *must* agree with the writer if he wishes to be considered a "reasonable person."

9. FOCUS ON THE ARGUMENT BEST CALCULATED TO PERSUADE YOUR READER.

The argument that you consider most impressive is not necessarily the one best calculated to persuade your reader. Different arguments will appeal to different readers. Just as it is important to understand and appreciate your reader's viewpoint, it is important to determine carefully which argument will be most appealing to one who holds that viewpoint. Let us take as an example one of the most heated and protracted controversies to have occurred so far in the second half of this century, the Vietnam war. The arguments that were used for and against American participation in that war may be classified as follows:

Classification	Arguments for U.S. Participation	Arguments against U.S. Participation
Moral and Religious	1. It is the moral obligation of the strong to protect the weak. 2. Communism is amoral and atheistic and must be defeated.	1. The Judeo - Christian tradition says to return good for evil, love for hate. 2. Modern methods of war are grossly immoral—they maim and scar combatants and noncombatants alike.
Political and Practical	1. We must win to "save face" and retain the confidence and respect of the free world. 2. We have an investment in American dollars and lives. 3. Our withdrawal would encourage the spread of Communism.	1. We are losing face by continuing in a war thousands of miles from our shores, a war we have been unable to win. 2. The war is too costly in terms of American dollars and lives. 3. Our withdrawal would encourage peaceful coexistence.
Philosophic	1. Free men must preserve the freedom of others.	1. The way to preserve a country's freedom is not by destroying the country and people.

When writers who supported U.S. participation in Vietnam wrote to challenge the position of the many clergymen who opposed participation, they frequently offered political and practical arguments. In doing so, they apparently failed to anticipate the clergymen's reaction, which can be summarized as follows: "There are, we admit, many political and practical reasons—but it is not the political and practical matters that should be paramount. It is the moral and religious!" It would have been much more effective for those writers to have chosen a moral or religious argument (for example, "It is the moral obligation of the strong to protect the weak"), since that was the context of the clergymen's argument.

Similarly, the wise writer who was addressing a group of history professors or members of governmental departments directly involved with the war in most cases would have emphasized not the moral or religious arguments, but the political and practical, or perhaps the philosophical. The point to keep in mind whenever you are writing a persuasive composition is that you will write most effectively when you choose the presentation that is most likely to persuade your reader.

10. NEVER USE AN ARGUMENT YOU DO NOT BELIEVE IS TRUE OR RELEVANT.

This principle should be understood as a qualification of principle 9. Absolute sincerity and regard for the truth are the most important characteristics of a writer. Without these there is no real persuasion, only "artful" presentation.

If, for example, a writer believed that U.S. intervention was a mistake because there was no chance of conducting the war except with modern methods of war, and if he were convinced that these methods were grossly immoral, and finally, if he were convinced that all the other arguments against U.S. intervention missed the real point, then in honesty he could not have emphasized the political and practical or philosophical argument to support his position. To be honest with himself and his readers, one must say what he really believes. He may, of course, sketch in the other arguments that he feels may impress his readers. But he must place these in the context of his real belief—that is, that only one argument is really significant.

The purpose of rhetoric is to present the truth. Therefore the writer of the persuasive composition, like the writer of any composition, will not descend to appeals to prejudice or the use of loaded words or any other propaganda device. He will appeal to reason rather than to emotion, realizing that emotional arguments may be momentarily successful at certain times and in certain situations, but that they ultimately will be recognized for their deceitfulness and will work to the writer's discredit. He will extend himself in an effort to conquer his own prejudices and preconceived notions, but he will refuse to compromise the truth, despite any seeming loss of effectiveness, *despite even the risk of failing to persuade his readers.*

An Unpersuasive Composition

The student chose to write a composition pointing out one or more of his complaints about the quality of the campus dining hall food and service. His reader was the dining hall manager, his task to impress the reader with his reasonableness and dispose him to reevaluate the performance of his staff.

DINING HALL DELIRIUM

Violates Principle No. 3 Doesn't seek common ground

There is continuous discussion taking place on this campus about the dining hall. The students are disgusted with the poor quality of the food and service, and the dirty dishes and silverware. As a student, I would like to point out the reasons for complaining.

Violates Principle No. 5 (Actually, it's overstated) Sarcasm offends reader

First, let us consider the quality of the food. The meat is either undercooked or overcooked. It is of such low quality that one wonders how it ever got on the market to be sold. The vegetables are completely tasteless, but this is all right because few students bother to eat them. Some students receive bonuses in their meals—such as hair in their soup or dead flies in their potatoes. These are only a few examples of how poor the food is.

No examples offered to support charge

Another complaint of students is the inefficient service. Because of the slow service, students often sit down to a cold meal. Many students have to skip their meals because they don't have time to wait. Some are driven to eat in local restaurants at extra expense.

*Actually suggests
bad* intention
*(How can writer
presume to know
intentions of staff
when even the
facts are in
question?)*
*Sarcasm offends
reader*
*Creates unfavor-
able impresssion
upon reader
(Judges adminis-
trators rashly)*
*Shows disrespect
toward reader.
Also implies that
students are right,
reader (and others)
are wrong. No ad-
mission that students
occasionally do em-
bellish on facts.)*

Perhaps the most common complaint is the dirty dishes and silverware the students are forced to use. I suppose everything goes through a dishwasher, but by some strange coincidence few things come out clean. However, the work staff don't worry about it—they just close their eyes to the dirt and pass the dishes and silverware on to the servers. Egg caked to the forks and pieces of meat stuck to the plate— it certainly raises a student's spirits when he's eating two meals for the price of one!

The question is, what can be done to correct these problems? Students have already issued their complaints to administrative officials, but this has done no good. These people appear to have turned their heads from the problem. It is clear that something must be done. A lot of revising is needed. But will there be any? You know as well as I do. NO!

How should the student have approached his subject and reader? First he should have realized that the dining hall manager must either be a dishonest man, caring little whether he runs the dining hall well or poorly, or a conscientious man, anxious to make his operation efficient and excellent. If the student were convinced that the manager is dishonest, he would have been wise *not to write the composition for that reader at all,* but perhaps for the administrator to whom the manager reported.

If, on the other hand, he were sure the manager is conscientious and experienced he would have had to acknowledge that (1) he is familiar with the frequency and exaggeration of student complaints that are almost a tradition on college campuses, and that (2) despite his efforts to find all the flaws in his operation, he is apparently unaware of several. If the student had examined carefully the complaints he thought were justified—the poor quality of the food, the dirt in the food, the slow service, and the dirty dishes and silverware—he would have realized that they embrace the entire operation. Mentioning *all* of them was saying that nothing about the dining hall is acceptable—and such a comprehensive statement would surely have disposed the reader to reject the entire statement. His natural (human) reluctance to see the faults in his operation would not have been overcome, but reinforced. He would think, "It's not possible that I've failed to see all these problems. This student must be just a complainer."

A Persuasive Composition

The student skilled in persuasive writing would have anticipated all these reactions from his reader and have written his composition in this manner:

TEMPEST IN A TEAPOT

What type of student constantly complains about the quality of food in the dining hall? Usually the one who's been catered to by his mother and finds it difficult to adjust to anything but dotingly personal service. During the first term in college my roommate was just such a person. He moaned for an hour after every meal he ate here (and he went without more than a few meals). Hamburger steak was "unfit for human consumption" in his view. Chicken a la king was "slop." And so on—there was an appropriately derogatory comment for every meal he forced himself to eat.

John stayed here for about a month. He enjoyed his courses and did well in them. He made quite a few friends. But he came to speak constantly of his mother's cooking—two-inch steaks three times a week, lasagna, spaghetti with pork chops *and* meatballs *and* hot Italian sausage. So he left college to return to Utopia. Few students go as far as John did, of course, but judging by the frequency of the complaints I hear students make about the dining hall, he was not the only student hopelessly spoiled by his mother's cooking.

The service and quality of the food in our dining hall are usually good. Sure, the meat is occasionally overcooked, the vegetables are sometimes soggy, but that happened at home too (and my mother only cooked for five, not fifteen hundred). There are, in fact, only two things that I think might be improved.

The first is waiting in line. I usually have to wait at least fifteen minutes to be served in our dining hall, and I arrive quite early. I know from friends in other colleges that a fast-moving line is the exception rather than the rule, so perhaps nothing can be done about it. But if the management found some way to "stagger" the serving or speed up the line, at least one student would appreciate it. The second is dirty dishes and silverware. At most meals I find that I have to wipe dirt from at least one plate or piece of silverware. It may be that in the interests of efficiency the dishwashers are reluctant to wash dirty pieces a second time. Or they may be too busy to notice. But spotless dishes and silverware do help to make the food more appetizing.

Neither improvement would satisfy students who, like John, are spoiled or who enjoy complaining. But they would help to make our dining hall an even better place to eat.

The difference between these two compositions should be obvious. The most conscientious, eager-to-please dining hall manager could not help discounting the first as an exaggerated "blast" written by a chronic complainer or as a release of hostilities by a student angry not only with the dining hall staff, but with his girl friend, his professors, his parents, and the world. But any reasonably conscientious dining hall manager could not help but regard the second as the work of a reasonable, understanding, mature student. It would make him want to improve the service. In other words, it would be *persuasive*.

Knowing the Reader

As was noted in the beginning of this essay, it is more instructive to consider the reactions of readers with opposing views than those of readers who share our views, since the former offer a greater challenge to be reasonable. But the question remains, how do we go about determining what our reader thinks? How can we tell his thinking on the particular issue? How can we predict the subtle turns of mind that his experiences, matters closed to our knowledge, will make him take? The answer is that we can never do so with certitude. All we can do is consider what clues to his position are available, and try to build our understanding on them. The persuasiveness of our writing often depends on how sensitive we are to small clues. Sometimes the clues are very small indeed. But the skillful writer realizes the importance of reading them carefully. The basic situations we must deal with and the way to approach each—*before we write*—are as follows:

a) *If our reader is one who has written something we have read and disagree with*, we should re-read it very carefully and then jot down a summary statement of his position and a listing of his main points. Next we should ask ourselves what his position reveals about his thinking. Is there anything in what he has written that gives a clue about his attitude toward other matters related to his position but not specifically mentioned by him? Then we should jot down what we think is right with his position (what a reasonable person would be forced to accept), what is wrong with it, and how we can present our response persuasively. We should not be surprised if in reading the other person's writing, we discover that he violates one or more of the principles of persuasion. Rather, we should realize that since it is we who understand these principles, and therefore have a certain advantage over him, it is we who have the obligation to follow them.

b) *If all we know of our reader is that he is in general disagreement with our position,* we should ask what thinking might underlie his position, what his major specific objections might be, what evidence and reasoning he would probably offer in support of his position if he were discussing the issue with us. We should anticipate his response to each of our points. One of the best ways to do this is to review the essay "Reasoning," particularly the sections "Impediments to Sound Reasoning," and "Important Distinctions in Reasoning," asking what impediments the reader might have and what distinctions he may tend to overlook. This type of analysis, of course, can slip very easily into empty speculation. But we needn't worry about this if we really know the issue and have noted with care the various views that have been expressed concerning it.

Consider, for example, this writing situation. The topic is abortion. Our position is that it should be permitted in either of two circumstances: when the woman has been raped or when the pregnancy will seriously damage her mental or physical health. The only thing we know about our reader is that he opposes abortion on any grounds. If we have studied the issue closely, we will know that well-reasoned opposition to abortion usually focuses on one of the two premises: the theological premise that the authority to take the life of a human being (in this case, the fetus) belongs only to God, not to man; the philosophical argument that the highest purpose of the law is to protect the innocent, particularly the defenseless. We should acknowledge the probability that one of these premises, or both, is central to our reader's position. Thus we can proceed with the inquiry suggested in the previous paragraph in light of this probability.

3

Other Elements
of Rhetoric

SUBSTANCE

1. *Purpose in Writing*

Before we begin any piece of writing, we should be clear about our purpose in writing. Purpose is the end we wish to achieve, the particular effect we wish the piece to have. Which of our assertions need special explanation? Is any evidence needed? If so, what kind? What type of interpretation is called for? What techniques of analysis, if any, should we use? What should the scope of the piece be? What should be its focus? How should it be organized? These and the host of other questions that arise whenever we write can be answered only in terms of our purpose in writing. The main general purposes in nonfictive writing are these:

1. To inform the reader of factual data—for example, the details of the outbreak of hostilities in a small Asian country
2. To share experiences, our own or someone else's, with the reader by re-creating them as dramatically as they occurred
3. To dispose the reader favorably toward a particular point of view about something—for example, a book or film, the activities of a private or public agency, a prevalent habit or attitude, a current controversial issue
4. To arouse the reader to action

The latter two purposes are, of course, the ones that underlie persuasion. They differ from the first two in that they depend more for their effectiveness on an understanding of the audience.

At times our purpose in writing may be simply to inform or to share experiences. More often it will be a combination of two or more of the four listed above. For example, it may be to inform the reader of facts and arouse him to action, or to share an experience and dispose him to a viewpoint. Usually we will wish one purpose to dominate; therefore we will have to decide how most effectively to subordinate the other purposes to it.

The four purposes explained above represent writing-to-*convey*-a-message. Another very common purpose is writing-to-*discover*-a-message. In such writing we examine an issue, reviewing bits and pieces of fact and experience to stimulate our thinking, exploring various lines of reasoning, and searching for the most significant interpretation, the deepest meaning, the most comprehensive statement. Such writing is highly tentative and speculative. It is often scribbled cryptically in a personal shorthand only we can read. We jot down a thought, then another, then a qualification of the first; we cross out a part, then rapidly make several two or three word notes as several ideas come to mind in a rush. We fill the margins with questions about our jottings—"Is this really so or only apparently so?"; "Am I assuming something here?"; "What evidence do I have?"; "Just how significant is this point?"; "Does this contradict what I say above?" Moreover, we permit ourselves some moves that we would not approve in an outline or a draft of a composition, such as consciously going off on a tangent, dropping one thought abruptly and pursuing another, letting our comments range over the issue at random. In short, such writing is messy, redundant, and disorganized because its purpose is not communication but discovery. It is not written for any reader but ourselves and is seldom shown to anyone. But it can serve as effective preparation for writing that we do intend to be read by others.

2. Competency

Recognizing our competency involves accurately measuring what our various experiences, actual or vicarious, will permit us to judge and what not. It is all too easy to pretend that we have the competency required to make a particular judgment when in fact we do not; easiest, indeed, in matters about which we are very nearly ignorant. Our ignorance perhaps makes us uneasy and we compensate by feigning knowledge. For example, we may find ourselves saying, "The problem with most juvenile delinquents is that they think they know everything and therefore will not listen to people who could help them." After we have expressed the judgment and perhaps attempted without success to defend it, we may realize that, having never met a single delinquent and having read next to nothing on the subject, we are incompetent to speak.

What should give us greater pause than our recognized incompetency is our *un*recognized. It is a good habit to ask ourselves before we begin writing (or speaking) about any subject, "What is the extent of my competency? What type of judgments should I refrain from attempting?"

3. Fact and Opinion

A fact is something there is compelling reason to believe is so, something virtually closed to question or dispute. We say that something is a fact when our own experience or the verified report of others' experience is sufficient to exclude reasonable doubt. An opinion, on the other hand, is something we believe is so mainly through personal judgment and without compelling reason. We say that something is an opinion when our own experience or the verified report of others' experience is not sufficient to exclude reasonable doubt. Consider these statements:

1. In the mid-nineteen sixties there were outbreaks of violence in a number of American cities.
2. Many people believed those outbreaks were signs of "racial unrest."
3. Some people believed those outbreaks were caused solely by Negroes' anger over the injustices they have suffered because of discrimination against them.
4. Some people believed those outbreaks were caused by the essential lawlessness of Negroes.
5. The solution to the problem of violence in American cities is to increase the size of police departments.
6. Violence is learned behavior.

Statements 1 through 4 are factual; statements 5 and 6 opinions. However, 2, 3, and 4 are made factual only by the words "many (some) people believed"; if these words were omitted, each of these statements would be considerably more open to dispute, enough so in fact that they would more accurately be called opinions.

To say that a statement is an opinion does not mean it is false; it merely means that its truth or falsity is not certain. Similarly, to say that statements of opinion are more open to challenge does not mean that we should refrain from judging issues and forming opinions. It is hardly possible, after all, to think without making judgments; and thinking is surely desirable. What it means to say these things is that, since opinion is more open to challenge than fact, we should include in any piece of writing no more opinions than we can support adequately.

At times the writing situation will pose a more complex problem. We may be stating something that we know is a fact but that, because it is not widely known, the reader may interpret as our opinion. In such a case we should take special care to convince the reader it is factual by identifying the source from which we obtained it and perhaps providing some pertinent details about the source.

4. Assertions

Assertions are statements. They are not simply subjects, but subjects and predicates, complete sentences that declare something. There are several ways of classifying assertions. The first, as facts or opinions, was discussed in the previous section. A second is as *stated or implied*. "Robert Kennedy was assassinated in 1968," "That was the most boring novel I've read this year," and "I'm going to eat at Charlie's house tonight" are all stated assertions: they say just what their author means. However, the Yiddish proverb, "The girl who can't dance says the band can't play," is an implied assertion; it says one thing and means another. When a teacher quotes it to a failing student who has just criticized his teaching, he is saying, "The student who can't learn says the teacher can't teach." Similarly, "Oh, the long hours students spend studying—to hear students tell it," implies that students exaggerate about the time they spend studying. And "Their 'patriotism' moved them to beat the flag-burners" implies that what is called patriotism in this case may not be.

Another way of classifying assertions is by their *function* in a piece of writing—that is, by their importance. The central assertion is that which contains the main idea governing the piece of writing; secondary assertions are those that, directly or indirectly, develop or refine the central assertion. A fourth way is by the *degree of complexity*. Some assertions, even central assertions, may be very simple. A film reviewer, for example, may build his review of a film on no more complex an assertion than "This film deals rather effectively with the ludicrousness of old lechers." Yet other assertions may be very complex—that is, they may have more than a single part requiring further explanation or development. Here is an example of a complex assertion. "It is crucial for those who would deal effectively with young people to appreciate that although the young today generally regard such abstract nouns as 'faith,' 'authority,' 'tradition' less reverently than their parents did, and although they are more used to rapid change and therefore more open to innovation in every area of human affairs, they nevertheless share their parents' desire for self-knowledge and meaningful lives."

Whether they concern fact or opinion, are central or secondary, or more or less complex, our stated [1] assertions will communicate the meaning we intend only if we

a) Specify both subject and predicate clearly and accurately. We should not be content referring to "college students" when we mean "two fellows in my history class." Similarly, we should be careful to predicate about our subject no more and no less than what we intend. And this applies not only to our choice of verbs, but to our choice of tense and mood as well. Consider, for example, how the meaning is altered as the form of the verb changes in the following sentences.

War *has been* avoided.
War *can be* avoided.
War *must be* avoided.
War *should be* avoided.
War *could be* avoided.
War *will be* avoided.

b) Avoid ambiguity of time, place, circumstance, frequency. Are we saying that something is so now, was so in the past or will be so in the future? Is it so in all places or certain places? In all circum-

[1] The points that follow do not apply to implied assertions, which communicate indirectly and depend largely on the reader's ability to see through or beyond explicit statement.

stances or in certain ones? And how frequently? Always? Sometimes? Seldom? We can expect the reader to read only the qualifications we provide.

c) Say no more than we can develop and refine adequately in the space we have available. If the scope of our writing is to be modest, we should make our assertion appropriately modest.

Perhaps the most important point to recognize about assertions is that they not only more or less fulfill obligations to our reader, they usually *create* obligations to be fulfilled. Some assertions, of course, are self-fulfilling. Saying, "Mistakes can be learning experiences," "It rained last Tuesday," or (in la Rochefoucauld's words) "As it is the characteristic of great minds to express much in few words, so small minds have the gift of speaking much and saying nothing," creates no real obligation. But saying (with St. Bernard), "Everyone is his own enemy," creates an obligation to explain in what sense "enemy" is to be understood. Saying to someone who has never heard it before, "The square of the hypotenuse of a right triangle is equal to the sum of the squares of the sides" creates the obligation to present evidence (in this case demonstration) that the assertion is so. Saying, "An inordinate preference for one's own opinion leads to an undervaluing of facts" creates the obligation both to specify at what point such preference becomes "inordinate" and to show how it leads to an undervaluing of facts. And saying, "Our whole educational enterprise is founded upon the wholly false premise that at some prior stage the essential educational work has been done" [2] creates two sizable obligations—demonstrating that the whole enterprise is founded upon that premise and that the premise is wholly false.

Whenever we make any assertion, we should be aware of the obligations it creates and be prepared to meet them. Sections four through eight detail various ways they may be met.

5. Explanation

Explanation is clarification. It is required whenever an assertion leaves the reader uncertain of the full meaning intended by the writer. The need for explanation does not suggest a flaw in the assertion. (Such a flaw would, as pointed out in section three, de-

---

[2] William Arrowsmith, "The Heart of Education: Turbulent Teachers," *Matrix* '67, published by *Motive*, 1967, p. 12.

mand revision of the assertion, not explanation.) It suggests merely that the idea cannot be adequately presented by assertion alone.

There are two ways to explain—by expanding the assertion and by interpreting it. The following passage is an example of the former. Note how the second and third sentences amplify the first.

> . . . If, a century from now, the social historian should read many best sellers of our time, he would be forced to conclude that male and female Americans of this period were wholly engaged in amorous and extramarital affairs, with incidental excursions into business, politics, war, and so forth. For nowadays affairs are as automatic in a novel as corpses in a detective story; the only question is how many are required. The emotional and moral tension that might be set up by an effort at self-control hardly comes into the contemporary view of human nature.[3]

The more common way of explaining is by interpreting. Consider, for example, the assertion "God is dead." What does it mean? If we interpret it literally, we conclude that it means, "There is no Supreme Being who is distinct from the world yet responsible for its existence and providential in His relation to it." But if we read it figuratively, we may choose from a number of interpretations:

> Man no longer *wants* to believe God exists.
> Man is no longer *able* to believe God exists.
> Man is no longer *certain* God exists.
> Man no longer *acts* as if God exists.
> Man no longer *cares* if God exists.
> Man no longer accepts some particular conception of God.
> Man is no longer satisfied with the limitations of traditional human expressions of belief in God's existence.

If the writer who makes this assertion wishes to have his meaning understood, he must provide the reader with the interpretation he intends. To leave the reader to his own interpretation is, in this case, to be almost certain of failing to communicate.

Here is another example of explanation by interpretation. Notice that the assertion in sentence one creates two obligations for explanation—in what way did Schweitzer help make it possible and in what way was the moral vision blocked? Since the second question addresses the prior condition, the author considers it first; thus

[3] Douglas Bush, "Sex in the Modern Novel," *The Atlantic*, January, 1959, p. 73.

sentences two and three interpret the idea of a blocked moral vision. Sentence four interprets Schweitzer's contribution.

> The main point about Schweitzer is that he helped make it possible for twentieth-century man to unblock his moral vision. There is a tendency in a relativistic age for man to pursue all sides of a question as an end in itself finding relief and even refuge in the difficulty of defining good and evil. The result is a clogging of the moral sense, a certain feeling of self-consciousness or even discomfort when questions with ethical content are raised. Schweitzer furnished the nourishing evidence that nothing is more natural in life than a moral response, which exists independently of precise definition, its use leading not to exhaustion but to new energy.[4]

6. Evidence

Beyond making an assertion and providing necessary explanation lies the largest part of the writing process, largest both in the sense of the space it occupies and in the sense of the time the writer spends doing it. That part is providing evidence, supporting the assertion. Assertion merely tells the reader something; evidence *shows* him. Therefore, his reaction to a piece of writing is strongly influenced by the amount and quality of the evidence presented.

What is the "right" amount of evidence? It varies from situation to situation, depending on the assertion and the audience. The writer who learns to appraise accurately the impact of what he says will have little difficulty knowing how much evidence to present. It is likewise impossible to speak definitively of the "right" quality of evidence, since different situations will demand different types of evidence. However, it is possible to classify the main types of evidence broadly, in the order of their relative effectiveness.

Very Effective   1. First-hand comprehensive experience or observation—what we have not only been involved in or witnessed, but know considerable background information about
2. First-hand experience or observation—what we have been involved in or witnessed but know little or no background information about
3. The testimony and evidence presented by authorities

[4] Norman Cousins, "What Matters About Schweitzer," *The Saturday Review*, September 25, 1965, pp. 30-31.

Effective	4. Verifiable report—the experiences and observations of others (especially those we know are trustworthy) in matters that can be verified, most news reports in the various media (in substance if not in every detail), evidence presented by writers of good reputation who are not authorities on the subject
Ineffective	5. Unverifiable report—the experiences and observations of others (especially those whose trustworthiness we are uncertain about) in matters that cannot be verified, news reports from non-standard agencies, evidence presented by writers of questionable reputation

The reason personal experience and observation are placed first in the order of effectiveness is that they represent the type of evidence we can speak about most authoritatively and with the least possibility of distortion. There are, of course, numerous writing occasions when our experience and observation are of little use. In doing a paper on the causes of the Thirty Years' War for a history course, we would probably support our assertions exclusively with the testimony of authorities on that subject. Yet there are many occasions when our own experiences are relevant to our assertions. And on such occasions it is well to realize that even the smallest, seemingly most insignificant incident can be effective when handled skillfully. As one well-known writer observed,

Very few of us ever see the history of our own time happening. And I think the best service a modern journalist can do to society is to record as plainly as ever he can exactly what impression was produced on his mind by anything he has actually seen and heard on the outskirts of any modern problem or campaign. Though all he saw of a railway strike was a flat meadow in Essex in which a train was becalmed for an hour or two, he will probably throw more light on the strikes by describing this which he has seen than by describing the steely kings of commerce and the bloody leaders of the mob whom he has never seen—nor any one else either. If he comes a day too late for the battle of Waterloo (as happened to a friend of my grandfather) he should still remember that a true account of the day after Waterloo should be a most valuable thing to have. Though he was on the wrong side of the door when Rizzio was being murdered, we should still like to have the wrong side described in the right way.[5]

[5] G. K. Chesterton, "The Conscript and the Crisis," *A Miscellany of Men* (London: Methuen & Co. Ltd., 1912), pp. 129-30.

When we need evidence other than our experience, in most cases we can obtain it reasonably quickly if we approach the job of re-searching systematically. The following is one simplified approach:

1. Consider the various headings under which the subject might be listed. Consult a good encyclopedia and read the articles under those headings, making notes as necessary and noting the bibliography listed at the end of each entry.
2. Consult the library card catalog under the appropriate general headings and the specific titles (authors) found in the encyclo-pedia bibliographies. Note the books available. Consult the ap-propriate periodical indexes. (The librarian will be able to direct you to any special holdings—pamphlets, bulletins, etc.—that per-tain to the subject.) Note relevant articles.
3. Obtain and consult the articles you have listed. Before you read a work, scan it, checking the table of contents and index to de-termine if it contains anything useful. Do not waste time read-ing what does not pertain to your topic. Check the footnotes and bibliographies of books you find helpful—they may suggest other helpful sources. As you read, make notes citing page numbers and indicating (for your own later reference) whether you are quoting or paraphrasing.

7. Techniques for Presenting Evidence

a. Reporting

This technique is commonly associated with the presentation of news stories in the various communications media. In addition to this use, it serves to present the approaches and findings of research and to translate statistical data from graphs and charts into words, as in this passage:

Research psychologist Richard H. Blum, at Stanford University's In-stitute for the Study of Human Problems, went to the source to learn who takes drugs and why. Dr. Blum and his associates interviewed at random 200 persons, young and old, living in the San Francisco Bay area. Their interviews painted a composite of the kind of people who are heavy drug users.

They are more often white than Negro, and they are better edu-cated, divorced more often, earn more money and have fewer political ties than the average person. Also, they rebel against au-thority and frequently express dislike of their parents, themselves, and their work. Heavy users reveal strong likes and dislikes, are compulsive about their activities and show numerous signs of inner conflicts. They use drugs for religious motives or for self-analysis. As a group, they told of frequent use of medicinal drugs during childhood.

Dr. Blum concludes that those students and adults who turn to LSD, marijuana and pills are "inner" people; those who do not abuse drugs, he calls the "outer" people. Inner people concentrate on the thoughts that swirl within their heads. Outer people look to external experiences, what's happening around them.[6]

Reporting is also used to present significant or interesting details about a subject briefly and straightforwardly, as in this passage:

When Lew [Alcindor] was 13, and obviously still growing, a flock of prep schools began offering him scholarships. Lew's father, a New York transit policeman, is a Catholic, as is his mother, and the Alcindors decided to send their only child to Power Memorial Academy, a small parochial school on Manhattan's West Side.

At Power, Alcindor came under the control of Coach Jack Donohue, a stern young man who was already acquiring a reputation as one of the best coaches in the city. Donohue brought Alcindor along slowly. As a freshman the boy was too awkward to do much but wave his long skinny arms and dunk an occasional basket. But by his sophomore year, when he was 15 years old and nearly 7 feet tall, Alcindor was agile enough to make the high-school All-American team and to lead Power to an undefeated season.

From then on he simply got better. Some rival coaches used to whisk their teams off the floor before Power warmed up so that their players would not see him any sooner than they had to. Wearing size 16D shoes and sucking a lollipop, Alcindor would loosen up by starting his leaping lay-ups from somewhere around the foul line. Then he would casually dunk the ball with either hand, to the delight of the fans.

When reporters and photographers began to hound Alcindor, Donohue protected his boy in his usual forthright fashion. He simply ordered Lew to talk to no member of the press, and the arrangements suited Lew fine. He was ill at ease talking to adults, perhaps because he towered over them. Frustrated photographers began stalking him as though he were a skittish giraffe. Once, after ducking into a subway to escape, Alcindor told a friend that it was all becoming like cops and robbers. "People want you not for yourself," Donohue warned him, "but because you're a basketball player. Don't forget that." [7]

[6] Roland H. Berg, "Why Americans Hide Behind a Chemical Curtain," *Look*, August 8, 1967, p. 13.

[7] Rex Lardner, "Can Basketball Survive Lew Alcindor?" *Saturday Evening Post*, January 14, 1967, p. 71. Reprinted by special permission of *The Saturday Evening Post*, © 1967 by The Curtis Publishing Company.

In reporting, the emphasis is on objectivity, leaving the opinions of the reporter out, avoiding slanting as much as possible, simply presenting the facts.

b.   Brief Illustration

The brief illustration may be a quick reference to a case-in-point, a simple listing of a number of cases-in-point, or a summary of an incident. It is usually a paragraph or less in length. The details it includes, if any, are only the essential ones, those that are directly relevant to the assertion it supports. It particularly omits details of time and place that are irrelevant to the writer's purpose, however interesting they may be, moving rapidly over them in the following manner:

> Space: Then after concluding their affairs in California, they drove to New York. When they arrived . . .

The details of the trip, which are not relevant, are omitted.

> Time: Joe Smith's coverage of the 1960 democratic campaign was complete. He traveled with the Kennedy team over every grueling mile, heard every speech. But in the 1964 campaign, except for three or four brief trips with Johnson, he remained at his desk in New York.

There is a jump of four entire years between sentences—because those years are not related to the point being made.

Quick Reference to a Case-in-point (Note that most of the sentence is an assertion. The last eight words refer to the case-in-point.)	When a dignitary from a foreign country, even from a country hostile to our ideals visits the United States, our communications media are intent on capturing his every word and gesture, as they were when Kosygin visited in 1967.
Simple Listing of a Number of Cases-in-point (The first two sentences are assertions, the rest of the passage is the simple listing.)	Over the centuries a hero has been a man, a woman, a child, a dog, a goat— a single entity. The curious fact about today's heroes is that they are not singular but plural. . . . There are Rover Boys; the Hardy Boys; Jack, Doc and Reggie; the Lone Ranger and Tonto; Marshall Dillon and Chester; Christopher Robin, Winnie-the-Pooh and Piglet; Na-

polean Solo and Illya Kuryakin; Buck
Rogers, Wilma and Doctor Zarkoff; Mandrake
and Lothar; Lamont Cranston and
Margot Lane; Perry Mason, Paul Drake
and Della Street; and Henry Aldrich and
Homer—just to name an even dozen.[8]

*Summary of an Incident
(Note that the Webster-Clay
anecdote contains only the
crucial issue of the case, and
that the larger part of the
illustration is given to creating
the suspense before Webster's
reply.)*

[My grandfather] was noted for his dry
wit and I could listen to his anecdotes
for hours. One I shall never forget was
a patent case with Daniel Webster and
Henry Clay as the opposing attorneys.
Webster pleaded that a certain machine
violated the patents rights of his client.
Clay denied this, and his eloquence held
the court breathless for hours until one
would have thought that the two machines
no more resembled each other
than day and night. When Webster rose
to answer, the stillness was profound,
the excitement intense. Millions of dollars
hung in the balance. He gravely
placed the two machines before the jury,
saying, "There they are. If you can see
any difference between them it is more
than I can," and sat down. He won the
case. And my grandfather had illustrated
a lesson which unhappily, I have not always
emulated: "Never talk more than
is necessary." [9]

The serious writer is observant and develops skill in recalling
relevant incidents. He sees the writing possibilities in his encounters
with the supercilious men's store clerk and with the clumsy waiter
in the cheap restaurant, and in his observations of the foolish
woman shopper pretending to be four sizes smaller than she really
is, his small son's expert taunting of big sister, his dachshund's habit
of barking viciously when a strange dog appears and then running
away if the other dog accepts the challenge. And he draws on them
when they serve his purpose, just as he draws on his reading and
television-watching.

Similarly, the serious writer makes himself be a good *listener*.
When his friends and acquaintances are relating what has hap-

[8] James Lincoln Collier, "The Multiple Hero," *Holiday*, April, 1967, p. 10.
[9] Douglas MacArthur, *Reminiscences* (New York: McGraw-Hill Book
Company, 1964), p. 5.

pened to them or what they have seen, he realizes that what they are saying may provide him with illustrations for writing. What he does not understand clearly or what is incompletely told, he asks the speaker to repeat or clarify. Always as he listens, he attempts to evaluate the story, determine what conclusions can be drawn from it, and relate it to his own experiences and observations.

The most common error in brief illustration is loss of focus, getting so involved with the illustration that we forget the assertion it is supporting. No matter how interesting the case itself may be, if we decide to use it in a brief illustration, we should include only those aspects of it that are relevant to the assertion.

c. Extended Illustration

There are occasions when brief treatment will not do justice to the incident being related, cases in which more detailed treatment will increase the effectiveness of the illustration. On such occasions we use extended illustration, or as it is frequently termed, narration. Like brief illustration, extended illustration deals with a particular case-in-point used to support an assertion. It is, however, at least a paragraph in length, usually longer. It can, if very detailed, serve as the sole support of the assertion. In addition, it differs from brief illustration in the following ways:

1. Extended illustration tends to employ single direct quotations and dialogue more frequently than brief illustration does.
2. It includes more details of the incident than brief illustration does, and tends to include every step in the sequence of events rather than to summarize. It has few, if any, gaps in time and space.
3. It more frequently employs present tense, which creates a sense of immediacy.

Here are some examples of extended illustration:

The incident is related here step-by-step, with no action omitted. Note that, unlike many extended illustrations, this one lacks dialogue, has little direct quotation, and uses past tense. The choice to use or not use these devices depends on the par-

Standing near the edge of the antarctic ice, Herbert Ponting, official photographer of the British Terra Nova Expedition, was focusing his camera on a group of killer whales out in the bay. Suddenly the three-foot-thick ice heaved up under his feet and cracked. There was a loud blowing noise, and Ponting was enveloped in a blast of hot, acrid air that *ticular effect the writer wishes to achieve.*

smelled strongly of fish. Eight killer whales had come up under him, broken the ice with their backs and isolated him on a small floe. Now the floe began rocking furiously, and the whales shoved their huge black-and-white heads out of the water. One ugly tooth-filled snout was within 12 feet.

The photographer leaped to a nearby floe, then to another and another. The killers followed him, literally snapping at his heels like a pack of hungry wolves. By the time Ponting gained the last floe it had drifted too far from the solid ice for him to make a jump. Then, by an extraordinary stroke of luck, currents pushed the floe back so that the gap was narrowed.

Still clutching his camera, Ponting made a life-or-death leap. His boots hit solid ice and he took off running. He glanced back just once. He saw, in his own words, "a huge, tawny head pushing out of the water and resting on the ice, looking around with its little pig-eyes to see what had become of me." [10]

The writer begins with a lead-in explanation, specifying his reason for offering the illustration. Then he explains the particulars of the assignment.

When Henry Brooke Carter died recently, the news stories in all the media included highlights from his long and distinguished career in journalism. But for those of us who studied journalism with him, the anecdote that will perhaps be longest remembered is the following one, which I offer here as a personal footnote to the record.

The assignment was to be done during the semester break and would serve as our lead-in to the second semester. There was almost a month to complete it—nevertheless it was difficult. We were to obtain an interview with someone who had just made the front page of a daily newspaper and write a lively account of the person's reactions to being in the spotlight. The instructor explained that

[10] William J. Cromie, "Killer Whale!" *The Reader's Digest*, March, 1963, pp. 176-77. Used with permission.

the person's story needn't have been glamorous—it could have been just a slender human interest affair. What was important was the person's reactions and how well we could commit them to words.

Here he recounts what happened after the semester break.

For most of us the vacation passed swiftly. When we returned to campus, a single question was on everyone's lips—"What did you get?"

The answers drew varying responses, from polite nods and ho-hum expressions to excited requests to explain every detail.

"What did you get?"

"Queen of the County Fair."

"Uh huh."

"How about you?"

"A man attacked by a pig."

"Really? Attacked? By a *pig*?"

And so on through a small catalog of events, many predictable, a few bizarre. But the one that earned the admiration and awe of all of us was Henry Carter's. For it revealed a preview of that rare combination of good fortune, nerve, and ingenuity that mark the superlative newsman. And we didn't have to ask him about it. We'd read about it in the papers.

Note the use of broken time order (flashback) here. The writer takes Henry's experience out of the natural sequence of events and places it at the end to give it emphasis.

Henry had spent the first three weeks of the semester break enjoying himself—skiing, dancing, playing ball. Only at the beginning of the fourth week did he begin to develop the slightest concern about the assignment, reading the newspapers every day but finding nothing that interested him. Then one day he was talking to a friend on a downtown corner of his city when a masked man ran out of a nearby bank and bumped into Henry. Reacting quickly, Henry grabbed the bandit's arm and twisted it, wrestling him to the ground and immobilizing him. The driver of a car that had apparently been waiting for the robber paused only

long enough to survey the situation.
Then he sped away. A moment later the
police arrived.

When the man was identified as a well-
known bank robber, wanted in several
states, Henry's face and story made national headlines. And Henry completed
the journalism assignment by interview-
ing *himself*.

Material for extended illustration, like that for brief illustration,
is most available to the writer who is observant and a good listener.
The most common error in extended illustration is faulty sequence,
the ineffective presenting of details out of the order in which they
occurred, jumping backward and forward in time unnecessarily.
This does not mean, of course, that one should not use flashback.
It means that he should not use it unless it is effective to do so.

d. Description

Description conveys sensory impressions—sights, sounds, smells,
tastes, touches. It makes our writing more lively and vivid and dis-
poses the reader more favorably to our conclusions by giving him
a mental image of the person, place, or thing we are speaking about,
letting him see, understand, appreciate, and react as we did.

The principal characteristic of description is the use of physical
detail arranged to give an overall or dominant impression—that is,
to reveal the distinguishing features of what is described. The
criteria by which the effectiveness of description is judged are
whether it makes a picture (in the broad sense, covering all the
senses) for the reader and how sharp, clear, and detailed that
picture is. In describing a thing we must keep in mind whether it
is likely the reader is familiar with it. If we were describing the
special features of a new model refrigerator, for example, we could
omit details about standard features. Or if we were describing a
smashed car, we could assume the reader knows what a car looks
like and focus exclusively on details of the damage. However, when
we are relatively sure the reader has never seen the thing, we are
obliged to include all important details. And if the thing is in an
unusual condition, we should describe its usual appearance as well
as its present appearance. We may, of course, blur certain features
of a person in order to highlight others, or blur certain features of

a place in order to convey the fact that our view was hazy or fleeting. Similarly, the requirements of the larger matter of the whole composition may be such that only partial description is possible. Despite these exceptions, however, it remains generally true that it is the arrangement of detail to give an accurate, effective sensory impression that constitutes excellence in description.

Describing People

This example describes a person as she usually appeared. Sometimes it is useful to describe someone as he appeared on a particular occasion.

She was about 5'9" tall and must have weighed at least 195 pounds. Her eyes were beady and very suspicious, her nose absurdly tiny for such a broad face. The corners of her mouth dipped in a perpetual frown, and her normal speaking voice was a low hiss. Her figure resembled a German tank on stilts—large and shapeless, with skinny, stick-shaped legs and big, long, flat feet.

Describing Places

Place description often depends for its effectiveness on how well we handle direction. Expressions like "to the right," "above," and "directly across from" help the reader see each detail in exact relation to other details.

Directly below my window a sidewalk stretches up to the parking lot behind the dormitory. To the right of the sidewalk a hill rises gradually to a broad plateau, bare except for an old barn made of rough-sawn lumber, its tin roof pitted with rust. To the left of the sidewalk, perhaps a half-mile up a gently sloping hill, is a large white frame farm house with a matching white barn. At the very top of the hill are dense woods.

Here direction is not so important. The focus is not on the arrangement of the furnishings but on their bizarre character.

His 12' by 5' room was originally planned to be a closet. The furniture consists of a sofa with three pillows and a 12" portable TV that refuses to work. Two hundred sixty beer cans are piled on top of one another to form a pyramid running the entire width of the room. A dozen mobiles made from popsicle sticks and empty "six-pack" cartons hang from the ceiling.

Describing Things

Here the writer can assume the reader is familiar with characteristics of statues in

Some [old statues in the Colombian Andes] consist of huge slabs with bas-relief carvings on the flat front and back *general and focus on the special features of these statues. Note that it is not a single statue that is described, but a whole class of statues.*

surfaces; others are simple cylindrical shapes on which a human or animal figure is outlined only superficially. Still others, carved in the round and using various planes, give proof of highly skilled workmanship and true mastery of form and material. Varying in body proportions and height—the tallest statues are about twelve feet—these stone carvings show a wide array of human and animal shapes or monstrous combinations of both. Squat human bodies with short, stiff limbs carry disproportionally large heads with feline features. Pointed fangs protrude from snarling jaws. There are warriors with helmets and clubs with secondary figures crouching on their heads, as if climbing over the backs of the statues. Others show females with elaborate headdresses, squatting animals, and a bird of prey holding in its beak and claws a writhing snake.[11]

Describing Impressions

Here accuracy of description demands not the differentiation of faces and clothing, but the blurring of them, for that is what was seen.

The train sped through the station. There were some people on the platform, perhaps a dozen. They all seemed mesmerized by the motion of the train. The speed at which we were moving blurred their features and transformed their clothing into a multi-colored ribbon.

Describing Thoughts

The writer used this description because it was an inaccurate depiction of college life—that is, because it permitted her to show (later) how mistaken she had been.

Before I entered college, my thoughts of college life were rather stereotyped—cobblestone paths; tall, dark, suave, handsome men speeding about in little red sports cars; distinguished professors graying at the temples, dressed in tweed, puffing on pipes, and speaking polysyllabically.

Describing Feelings

To the other patients the writer may have appeared calm as he sat in the dentist's

I had managed to forget my fear—until I heard the low moan from behind the door to the dentist's office. Then I grew

[11] G. Reichel-Dolmatoff, "Jungle Gods of San Agustin," *Natural History,* December, 1966, p. 41.

waiting room. But he didn't feel calm, and it is his feelings that he is describing here.

tense. My stomach ached. I felt very cold, yet perspiration was running down my forehead. "Make an excuse to the receptionist," I thought. "Just get out." I wanted to run. For the next twenty minutes I sat fixed to my chair, heart pounding, legs trembling.

Composite Description

This is the use of two or more types of description in the same passage. The writer records a combination of his sensory impressions of people, places, things, impressions, thoughts, and feelings, creating or re-creating a comprehensive sensory experience for the reader.

Here the approach is simple listing of details separated by commas and semicolons. Note that the brief and direct assertion (first sentence) governs the entire description. Note too the use of sentence fragments to keep the description fast-paced—"Smells," "People—masses of them!"; "Confusion, noise, smells, people. . . ."

My impressions weren't unique for a new arrival in Saigon. I was appalled by the heat and humidity which made my worsted uniform feel like a fur coat. Smells. Exhaust fumes from the hundreds of blue and white Renault taxis and military vehicles. Human excrement; the foul, stagnant, black mud and water as we passed over the river on Cong Ly Street; and overriding all the others, the very pungent and rancid smell of what I later found out was *nuoc mam*, a sauce made much in the same manner as sauerkraut, with fish substituted for cabbage. No Vietnamese meal is complete without it. People—masses of them! The smallest children, with the dirty faces of all children of their age, standing on the sidewalk unshod and with no clothing other than a shirtwaist that never quite reached the navel on the protruding belly. Those a little older wearing overall-type trousers with the crotch seam torn out—a practical alteration that eliminates the need for diapers. Young grade school girls in their blue butterfly sun hats, and the boys of the same age with hands out saying, "OK—Salem," thereby exhausting their English vocabulary. The women in *ao dais* of all colors, all looking beautiful and graceful. The slim, hipless men, many walking hand-in-hand with other men, and so misunderstood by the newcomer. Old men with straggly

Fu Man Chu beards staring impassively, wearing widelegged, pajama-like trousers. Bars by the hundreds—with American-style names (Playboy, Hungry I, Flamingo) and faced with grenadeproof screening. Houses made from packing cases, accommodating three or four families, stand alongside spacious villas complete with military guard. American GI's abound in sport shirts, slacks, and cameras; motorcycles, screaming to make room for a speeding official in a large sedan, pass over an intersection that has hundreds of horseshoes impressed in the soft, asphalt tar. Confusion, noise, people—almost overwhelming.[12]

The four most common errors in description are wordiness, vagueness, flowery phrasing, and intrusion of the writer. Wordiness is self-explanatory. It is caused most often by the writer's failure to rewrite and "tighten" his first drafts. Vagueness in description is the failure to *show* the reader rather than tell him; for example, substituting "he was an impressive man" for "he was a little over six feet tall and weighed over two hundred pounds; solidly muscled, he stood extremely erect, and walked in long strides, his feet seeming to spring from the floor."

Flowery phrasing is the use of ornate words, especially in a way that seems artificial or too emotional in the particular context—"it exuded a delicious fragrance" for "it smelled pleasant." And intrusion of the writer is the writer's frequent referring to himself or to his perspective ("I," "me," "my," "mine," "myself") so frequently or unnecessarily that he interrupts the description and distracts the reader. (It is, of course, sometimes necessary or useful for the writer to refer to himself in description; his presence is an intrusion only when it diverts the reader's concentration from what is being described.)

e. Figurative Definition

The term "definition" is usually associated with dictionary meaning—the literal, objective, essential description of how a word is

---

[12] Donald Duncan, "The Whole Thing Was a Lie (Memoirs of a Special Forces Hero)," *Ramparts,* February, 1966, p. 14. Copyright Ramparts Magazine, Inc., 1966. By Permission of the Editors.

used. (That type of definition is treated under "Techniques of Analysis.") Figurative definition is different. It is not literal, but literary; not objective, but subjective. It sometimes deals with the essential or most common meaning of a word, but more often with a secondary, incidental meaning, which from the specific viewpoint of a particular person or group may seem to be the sole meaning. The literal definition of "Thanksgiving," for example, is "an annual feast held in gratitude for divine favor." But to a young boy "Thanksgiving" means "golden brown turkey, cranberry sauce, steaming hot dressing, mashed potatoes and, gravy, freedom from having to eat vegetables, a table full of pies—apple and pumpkin, mincemeat and blackberry—cousins to play and share tales with, and a long, sleepy ride home in a crowded car." That is a figurative definition. It deals with the meaning of the holiday itself to a particular person rather than with the meaning of the word as most people use it.

Skillfully used, figurative definition can illuminate not only a word or an idea, but an entire point of view. The writer who sees not only his own emotional associations but those of others can present to his reader considerations the reader might otherwise miss, and help him understand and appreciate attitudes and views not his own. The words that lend themselves to figurative definition are those that concern people and their thoughts and feelings: names of people—Abraham Lincoln, Adolf Hitler, Robert Kennedy; names of places—Bethlehem, Paris, Moscow; words expressing virtues and vices—love, honor, patriotism, lust, war, murder; words denoting different religious, philosophical, political beliefs—communism, capitalism, Catholicism, Protestantism, Judaism, liberalism, conservatism, dogmatism; words referring to controversial issues—censorship, public welfare, secularism. Literal definition can provide valuable objective information and insights about the meanings of these words; but for information about the associations they have for people, we use figurative definition. Consider, for example, these literal definitions: [13]

> Nazism—the principles or methods of the Nazis
> Slavery—the condition of a slave; bondage
> Love—strong or passionate affection for a person of the opposite sex
> Mother—a female parent

[13] All taken from *The American College Dictionary* (New York: Random House, Inc., 1966).

United States—a republic in North America consisting of fifty states and the District of Columbia.

These definitions are clear and direct. They serve a useful purpose. But how different the definitions would be if they expressed the feeling of people for whom those words had strong personal associations—Nazism defined by a former inmate of one of the concentration camps that claimed the lives of nine million human beings; slavery defined by the descendant of an American slave; love by one experiencing its joys and pains; mother by a son or daughter; United States by a second world war hero.

Here are two examples of figurative definition:

Here the figurative definition of student protest, in terms of the associations it had for "many Americans," is divided into the initial reaction and the later one.

To many Americans in the mid-1960s student protest was a frivolity, a prank, the modern equivalent of flag-pole-sitting and goldfish-eating. Lines of students picketing an administration building to demand a voice in curriculum planning and campus regulations were to them cause more for laughter than for alarm. But as the lines grew longer and less orderly, the voices louder and accompanied by rocks and torches, to those same Americans student protest came to mean a threat to society, to civilization itself. As protest escalated, so did their response, until anyone of college-age who spoke of any grievance—no matter how reasonable the person nor how obvious the grievance—seemed to represent the forces of willful chaos.

Here the meaning of college for one individual is presented as a list of his activities.

To Joe, college means working out in the gym, speeding around town in his car, girl-watching in the student union, dancing and drinking every evening. It means spending his parents' money and all the change he can beg or borrow to gratify whatever urge happens to be shouting loudest at the moment. An exception, of course, is the urge to achieve academically, which he shows admirable skill in controlling, acknowledging it only by an occasional visit to class or the library, which more often than not, is given less to learning than to snoozing or to dreaming about his future success in business.

A common error in figurative definition is lack of clarity as to whose viewpoint the definition represents and what times, places, or conditions, if any, it is limited to. Another common error is unnecessary repetition of the "definition formula"—"it is" or "it means"; these words cannot, of course, be completely avoided, but they should not be used to the point of distraction.

f. Techniques in Combination

Seldom is any one of the above-mentioned techniques used as the sole technique in a piece of writing. In most cases two or more are used together, sometimes in simple sequential arrangement. The following passage is an example of such an arrangement, a movement from description to (in the last three sentences) illustration.

> Antonioni is a slight man of medium height. His wavy hair is well-combed, close to the head. He is always impeccably dressed, with a vague suggestion of formality and dignity about him. . . . If you did not know who he was, you would take him for . . . a Latin American gambler who frequents exclusive casinos.
> The chic gambler image is reinforced by his expression. He has bags under his eyes, which look weary under the half-closed eyelids. His deeply lined face is pale, sad, and patient. He looks as if he were endlessly waiting for something, the right number or the right card. His hidden anxiety is revealed by nervous tics: he turns his twitching face sideways at regular intervals and the twitching often serves him to gain a pause just before the delivery of a punch line. Once, one of his assistant directors, a man who owes him everything, said to a journalist that all he knew he had learned from his only master, the Japanese Akiro Kurosawa. Later the same young man needed a loan, and asked Antonioni for it. Antonioni looked at him with his bassethound expression and said: "You can go borrow money"—twitch, twitch—"from your master Kurosawa." [14]

In this case the author has used the illustration about the person to reinforce a descriptive detail. Similarly, a description of a place may precede an illustration of an incident that occurred there to help the reader visualize the incident in the real setting; or a figurative definition may precede (or follow) an extended illustration to help the reader appreciate the associations and attitudes the incident touched in the one who experienced it.

[14] Luigi Barzini, "The Adventurous Antonioni," *Holiday*, April, 1967, p. 100.

In addition to using the various techniques in simple sequential arrangement, a writer may *blend* two or more techniques. In such a blended passage one technique will usually dominate, the other(s) serving as the means by which it is achieved or as a way of enriching it. Of the numerous ways in which the techniques may be blended, the following are the most common:

Illustrative Description

Brief illustrations are used here as the writer's means of describing the scene. Each illustration presents a different activity, all of them occurring nearly simultaneously.

It might be the evening scene in any city slum. Unkempt youths clot the stoops of dilapidated tenements, talking over-boldly of drugs; drunks reel along gutters foul with garbage; young toughs from neighboring turf methodically proposition every girl who passes by, while older strangers hunt homosexual action. The night air smells of decay and anger. For all its ugly familiarity, however, this is not just another ghetto. This is the scene in San Francisco's Haight-Ashbury district, once the citadel of hippiedom and symbol of flower-power love.[15]

Descriptive Illustration

Here the illustration of the file of women is enriched by descriptive details of their peculiar motion and their appearance.

But what is strange about these people is their invisibility. For several weeks, always at about the same time of day, the file of old women had hobbled past the house with their firewood, and though they had registered themselves on my eyeballs I cannot truly say that I had seen them. Firewood was passing—that was how I saw it. It was only that one day I happened to be walking behind them, and the curious up-and-down motion of a load of wood drew my attention to the human being beneath it. Then for the first time I noticed the poor old earth-coloured bodies, bodies reduced to bones and leathery skin, bent double under the crushing weight.[16]

[15] *Time,* May 10, 1968, p. 31.
[16] George Orwell, "Marrakech," *Such, Such Were the Joys* (New York: Harcourt Brace Jovanovich, Inc., 1953).

Descriptive-Illustrative Definition

In this passage description and illustration are blended to achieve definition of several kinds—what the word "Appalachia" suggests, what the reality Appalachia means to people too busy to care, what the reality means to culture "buffs" who know only the stereotypes associated with their interests, and what the reality means to those who suffer it. (The device of examining something from the point of view of different observers, though especially useful in definition, can also serve as the framework for other techniques, such as simple description or illustration.)

Appalachia is a beautiful word. It trips off the tongue like the music of a murmuring primeval stream, full of peace and freshness. It evokes (in technicolor) an instant word-association montage of mountain mist and trails worn sleek by long-ago Indians, cherry blossoms, old women smoking pipes, and the family still out back.

Unless you've very recently been helping kids with their geography homework, you may not know exactly just what or where Appalachia is. Naturally it must be connected with the Appalachian Mountains—down south, isn't it, a little to the west, or is it the east? The name seems to keep cropping up in the papers and magazines, and you recall a TV documentary recently with Walter Cronkite talking about depressed areas in Appalachia, but you didn't listen very carefully because it was suppertime and the kids were making a racket.

Even if you *have* been reading the papers and know that it is the section between the Appalachian Mountain ranges, stretching north to Pennsylvania, down through Maryland, Virginia, Kentucky, the Carolinas, and northern Georgia, and that between nine and sixteen million people live there, perhaps the word has a more cultural than statistical meaning for you.

To you Appalachia may be that part of the country where dwell those beautiful characters of Jesse Stuart's fiction (what a master he is, he makes those people so believable!). Or maybe it is Martha Graham interpreting the Greek drama of an Appalachian spring in barefoot nuance to Copland dissonance. Of if you're a folk-song buff, maybe it means the carols of John Jacob Niles or those music festivals held in the hill country, in which the natives (called Dovie and Cora and Sister Della) sing

their hearts out in sad songs of Eliza-
bethan origin, and which will be taped
and sold as collector's items to city folk
who will exude admiration for these
people's clinging to traditions and their
stubborn pride in living as they please.
(There's where the true strength of
America lies, in its blue-grass roots!)
But to the people living in Appalachia,
the word means tragedy more than
poetry. It is a synonym for depressed
area—despair, lethargy and not just poverty but destitution. For one who has
grown up believing that the U.S. is the
best of all countries in its abundance of
physical goods, its gregarious principles
(in concept if not always in practice), its
concern for its children, its pride in its
almost luxurious standard of living, the
realization of what life is like right now
in Appalachia is like an icy, hard slap in
the face. It is running smack into Ten-
nessee Williams when you're thinking
Meredith Willson.[17]

How we combine the various techniques depends in a given
situation on our purpose in writing the piece, the purpose of the
particular part of the piece we are considering, and the kind and
amount of evidence we have to work with. But, as the above
examples indicate, the skill in combining techniques is one important mark of writing competency.

8. *Interpreting Evidence*

Whatever techniques we use and whether we use them singly
or in some combination, it is often necessary or helpful to clarify
the relationships between our evidence and our main assertions by
providing comments of interpretation. Consider, for example, this
paragraph of illustration:

Although all forms of cheating are offenses against intellectual integrity, some forms are more serious than others. Today one student

[17] Ethel Marbach, "Appalachia: A Witnessing for Christ?" *Ave Maria*,
July 25, 1964. Copyrighted material, used with permission.

in my class, tempted by the pressure of a difficult history exam, copied several answers from another student's paper. But last night a student in my dorm premeditatedly broke into the history professor's office, picked the lock on his file cabinet, and stole a copy of the exam.

The first sentence in this paragraph is an assertion. The two contrasting examples are clearly related to that assertion. But how much clearer and more forceful would the presentation be if this sentence of interpretation were added at the end?

The second student's offense was more serious because it was calculated and because it involved breaking and entering.

Such interpretation or comment is really minor assertion, telling the reader the writer's judgment about the evidence presented. It is usually a response to the natural questions the evidence suggests. These natural questions can be grouped according to the basic techniques used for presenting evidence.

Illustration

a) *Is the illustration completely typical or only partly so?* When we use an illustration that is partly typical, we create the obligation to explain in what way it is typical, in what way non-typical.

Ed may have loved everyone, as he so often claimed with apparent sincerity. But when someone said something to anger him, he answered by punching and kicking. One night he threw two students through a plate glass window after they had made a few negative comments about the Yankees. There are, I believe, many people like Ed, who accept brotherhood in theory but not in practice, *though surely few behave as extremely as Ed does.*

b) *Does the illustration really support the assertion?* At times we will use an illustration that we are unsure of. We may have good reason to believe it supports our assertion, but we are not certain that it does. Rather than pretend we are certain, we should offer our interpretation as a *tentative* one, sometimes including other possible interpretations.

Several of my professors spend from five to fifteen minutes each period talking about their wives, children, dogs, cats, cars—about anything but the subjects they are teaching. *Perhaps they do so to appear "human," perhaps to get the students' attention. I may be mistaken, but I think there is another, more reasonable explanation—that they are unprepared for class.*

Description

a) *Was the person, place, thing, etc. as it really appeared? Or was the appearance deceiving?* If the appearance described was deceiving, we will sometimes find it necessary to tell the reader in what way it was deceiving so that he is not misled.

> She was tall and slim. She spoke softly, gestured modestly, never ceasing to smile. Her every mannerism left no doubt that she was a gentle, refined person, a real lady. *Yet beneath this appearance she was not a lady at all, as I was soon to learn.*

b) *If the definition is understood and accepted by a particular person or group, but not by others, why have we selected it instead of other possible meanings?* This question usually arises not when we present two or more meanings, but when we present only one. However, even when we present only one, we do not necessarily create an obligation to add an interpretive comment. Sometimes the context will suggest the interpretation. When we feel it does not do so, or when we wish to reinforce the suggestion, we should add our interpretation.

> The term "God's Providence" at best is meaningless to an agnostic. It is an empty abstraction arising from the seemingly insuperable tendency of men to cling to superstition. At worst it is an ignorant mockery of the achievements of science, an excuse for apathy, an obstacle to human progress, an affront to the millions of suffering people who cry out, not for a transcendent "God" to "provide" what they need, but for their fellow man to share his bounty. *I mention this atheist's view not to suggest that it is theologically accurate, but to stress that it expresses a dissatisfaction with clichés, one that religious men should share.*

In answering the natural questions that arise from our evidence, we will, of course, not be showing, but telling our reader. And since telling is the *least* effective method of writing, we will therefore be most effective if we restrict our interpretations and comments to the absolute minimum and make them as brief as possible. When we recognize the need for comment, we should add it in the same paragraph as the illustration (or description, etc.), or if that paragraph is already rather long, comment in a separate paragraph.

9. Analysis

The writer who deals with complex or controversial issues has a special obligation to examine carefully the characteristics of his subject and its relations with other things because such issues are more difficult to understand than simple issues and because he must understand them to write effectively. The principles that guide the competent writer in analysis are listed below. The more closely we adhere to them, the more favorably our work is likely to be regarded by thinking people.

1. Take care that your reasoning is sound. (See "Reasoning.")
2. Never make an assertion you cannot support adequately, or that space limitations prevent you from supporting adequately.
3. Never oversimplify either a position you are attacking or your own position.
4. If the problem is too complex to admit of a "pat" answer, do not give a "pat" answer; show its complexity. If there is insufficient evidence to give an answer to the problem, do not attempt to give one.
5. Consider the consequences of your idea and ask whether they would all be desirable. If some would not, specify them and admit that they would not. (It is much more pleasant for a writer to identify the weaknesses of his position than to have a reader identify them.)

10. Techniques of Analysis

The various techniques of analysis discussed below are both methods of inquiry and of presenting the results of inquiry. That is, they may be used in writing-to-*discover*-a-message as well as in writing-to-*convey*-a-message.[18] For economy and convenience, they will be referred to here only in the second function, but in a way that will suggest an approach to the first.

a.   Definition

Definition in the non-figurative sense is, first of all, the literal, objective, essential description of the meaning(s) of a word as it

[18] The difference between these types of writing is explained in *Purpose in Writing*.

has been and is being used. It is helpful technique where we are using a term which we feel will be new to our reader, or where we are using a common word in an unusual way, or where formal definition is required by some larger purpose of our writing (for example, an evaluation of the way some people use or misuse a word). We begin definition of this type by placing the word in a general class and then noting the special features that differentiate it from other members of that class: a "monarchy" is a "form of government [general class] in which power resides actually or nominally in the ruler [differentiation]." Here is an example of this type of definition:

> Guerrilla tactics are those combative actions conducted by a smaller military force to defeat a larger one. The most common of these actions, all of which are designed to harass, terrorize, and demoralize the enemy, are ambushes, night raids, and mobilization of civilian (often peasant) populations.

It is well to remember that words have no meanings in *themselves*. Whatever meanings they have derive from the contexts in which people use them. And since today's contexts will be somewhat different from yesterday's, subtle changes in the meanings of words are going on all the time. This need not make us skeptical about the value of definition, however, since the changes occurring in our lifetimes will usually be relatively slight.

Another type of non-figurative definition is the identification of the inferences that may be validly drawn from a particular use of a word or a phrase. These inferences may concern the way the context shapes the meaning or the conscious or unconscious assumptions of the writer. Because of the impact of linguistic philosophy, in which it originated, this type of definition is frequently encountered in virtually every field of knowledge. The following is a non-technical example:

> The word "relevance" in its various forms has been very much in evidence on college campuses during recent years. Students speak of a particular lesson or classroom method or an entire course lacking "relevance" to their lives or their field of study. What they often seem to mean is not that the lesson or method or course has no significant bearing on their lives or field but that they *cannot see* its bearing. Apparently they regard "I can't see the connection" as synonymous with "There is no connection," without ever considering the possibility that to see the relevance of certain things one must

first learn them, and sometimes even wait several years until they can be synthesized with certain other things. Perhaps what many students are saying when they speak of relevance in this manner, whether they realize it or not, is that they refuse to place trust in the experience and judgment of their professors.

b. Process

Analyzing a process is explaining how something works or happens. It involves presenting the steps that are followed or occur, usually in exact, chronological order. This technique is used for diverse matters—providing instructions for assembling or servicing something (in which case the imperative is used, "Turn this: insert that."), detailing the way a scientific experiment is conducted, outlining the steps in the formation of habits or the passing of legislation or the writing of a composition. The first of the following examples briefly relates a historical process; the second is a more complete account of a phenomenon in nature.

The process of disintegration does not proceed evenly; it jolts along in alternating spasms of rout, rally, and rout. In the last rally but one, the dominant minority succeeds in temporarily arresting the society's lethal self-laceration by imposing on it the peace of a universal state. Within the framework of the dominant minority's universal state the proletariat creates a universal church, and after the next rout, in which the disintegrating civilization finally dissolves, the universal church may live on to become the chrysalis from which a new civilization eventually emerges.[19]

In theory, the step from water and carbon dioxide to the formation of sugar (the first result readily discerned) must involve several syntheses; yet it goes on in a split hundredth of a second. One sunlight particle or photon strikes the chlorophyll, and instantaneously the terribly tenacious molecule of water, which we break down into its units of hydrogen and oxygen only with difficulty and expense, is torn apart; so too is the carbon dioxide molecule. Building blocks of the three elements, carbon, hydrogen and oxygen, are then whipped at lightning speed into carbonic acid; this is instantly changed over into formic acid—the same that smarts so in our nerve endings when an ant stings us. No sooner formed than formic acid becomes formaldehyde and hydrogen peroxide. This last is poisonous, but a ready enzyme in the plant probably splits it as fast as it is born into harmless water and oxygen, while the formaldehyde is

[19] Arnold J. Toynbee, *Civilization on Trial* (New York: Oxford University Press, 1948).

877777777

knocked at top speed into a new pattern—and is grape sugar, glucose.[20]

c. Determination of Causes

This technique is the presentation of what we have found to be the causes of a phenomenon, those things which have influenced its existence, development, or (in the case of an event) occurrence.

> [Why is America violent?] I think there are two basic causes. In the first place, if millions of persons get accustomed to sitting down every afternoon and evening to watch films of the brutal killing of people, of unspeakable horrors, perhaps even having a drink with it—and then sleep well—this is a fact which makes them less and less sensitive to violence. It even infects them with a sense of violence as something normal. In this perspective the war in Vietnam and the threat of nuclear war have directly contributed to an underlying mood of violence which, in fact, has been increasing since the beginning of the First World War. That war, and then Hitler and Stalin, the bombing of Dresden and Coventry and Hiroshima—in all of this there has been an intense disregard for life which has created a mood of violence, a lack of sensitivity toward life, a lack of respect for life.
>
> But there is another cause, an element found in our whole mode of living in the United States. We profess the ideas of our traditional values of love, of truthfulness, of consideration, of individuality, of idealism but, in fact, we are one of the most materialistic cultures that exist. We accuse the Russians of their materialism, which is to be sure a perfectly true accusation, except that it has largely the function of projecting our materialism and saying "They are the bad ones."
>
> As a result of this materialism, I think we are getting more and more dehumanized—not in the sense of cruelty but in the sense of losing respect for individuality, for love, for all of the specifically human qualities which have been the content of our religious and humanistic traditions.[21]

d. Determination of Effects

This technique is the presentation of what we have found to be, or what we propect would or will be, the effects of a particular

[20] Donald Culross Peattie, *Flowering Earth* (New York: G. P. Putnam's Sons, 1939).

[21] Erich Fromm, "Why Is America Violent?" *National Catholic Reporter,* June 16, 1968, p. 5. Used with permission of *National Catholic Reporter* and the author.

phenomenon, those things or events whose existence or development the phenomenon has influenced.

True, we are in a revolutionary situation; true, Negroes demand justice "now." And equally true, we are reaping the grim harvest of white racism. But the answer does not lie in giving formal sanction to black racism. Nor dare we forget that community control in Harlem means community control in Queens and any other district with a distinct ethnic or religious composition. While an African curriculum will be fashioned in one school, the teaching of evolution may be dropped in another in accordance with local wishes. If the governing board in one section knows best what their children need, the same holds for a governing board with other ideas. If one board can fire white teachers, another can do the same to Negro teachers. If black berets will be legitimate school headdress, so will white hoods in another locality.

No rich imagination is required to foresee to what excesses caprice and bigotry, white and black, may lead. Once uniform standards for curricula, for promotion, and for teacher hiring can be superseded by local obscurantism or self-interest, the public-school system as a progressive and unifying force has been effectively destroyed.[22]

e. Analogy

Analogy is the explanation of the activities or characteristics of something unfamiliar to the reader by reference to something else with which he *is* familiar and which is similar in some way. Analogy is useful in situations where exactness is not demanded and the complexity of the thing being explained precludes direct explanation, or when an especially vivid explanation is desired. (Where exactness is demanded, analogy should not be used.)

A virus of any sort is lifeless until it attaches itself to a living cell, and gets its nucleic acid into the cell itself. Like the plane hijacker who diverts an aircraft from its intended destination to, say, Havana, the viral nucleic acid seizes control of the cell's manufacturing machinery. Within minutes or hours in different cases, the cell is diverted from serving its own needs to producing the components to form new viruses, reproducing the invader. The end of the process is the death of the "hijacked" cell and the appearance of hundreds of thousands of new viruses.[23]

[22] Marie Syrkin, "Don't Flunk the Middle-Class Teacher," *N. Y. Times Magazine*, December 15, 1968, pp. 88 ff.
[23] Harry Schwartz, "Medicine: 'Trying to Outsmart the Flu Virus,'" *N. Y. Times*, December 29, 1968, p. 9E.

f. Classification

Classification is breaking something down into its sub-groups according to some unifying idea. For example, an English professor might classify his books according to literary type—non-fiction, fiction, poetry, drama—or according to size—small, large, oversized. An automobile enthusiast might classify the latest car models according to performance, styling, or even safety features. It is important to be consistent in classifying—that is, to be certain that everything classified is covered by the unifying idea. Classification helps us to arrange things in a logical, orderly manner to facilitate closer examination using one of the other techniques of analysis (for example, comparison). It also helps us to inform our readers in what manner we will proceed with our analysis. Where the treatment of each thing classified is lengthy or the relationships unusually complex, classification is usually presented all at once in a separate paragraph, in this manner:

> The main elements of fiction are plot, the events of the story; character, the people to whom the events happen; setting, the place or atmosphere in which the story occurs; and theme, the meaning(s) the events suggest in context. We may analyze these separately to determine the contribution of each to the story, but we should remember that the story itself is more than the sum of the parts. It is the parts themselves plus the relationships among them.

However, where the treatment of each thing classified is relatively brief or the relationships not too complex (and occasionally even in a long, complex treatment), classification may be broken into several parts. If, for example, the above classification were so broken, the paragraph as it is written would dissolve; the reference to plot would introduce the discussion of plot, the reference to character, the discussion of character, and so on. The idea in the second and third sentences would be taken up at the end of the paper.

g. Comparison

Comparison is showing the similarities or dissimilarities (contrasts) between two things. Showing similarities poses few difficulties. We simply use an expression like "in both cases," "they looked alike," or "to both groups this means" and proceed to deal with the two cases as if they were one. But showing the dissimilarity is slightly more difficult. We must employ either an opposing or an alternating pattern. In an *opposing* pattern we complete the treatment of one thing before presenting the contrasting one. In an *alternating* pattern we contrast each detail of an illustration, description, or definition separately. Here is the same comparison shown in both patterns:

Opposing Pattern	*Alternating Pattern*
One man was tall, thin, and slightly stooped. He had a thick, unkempt mustache and long, straggly hair. His tweed sport coat was badly frayed, his trousers baggy, his shirt open. The second man was short and stocky, his posture erect. He was clean-shaven and nearly bald, and wore a neat blue pin-striped suit, a starched white shirt, and a tartan plaid tie.	One man was tall, thin, and slightly stooped; the other short and stocky, his posture erect. The first had a thick, unkempt mustache and long, straggly hair, and wore a badly frayed tweed sport coat, baggy trousers and an open shirt. The second was clean-shaven and nearly bald and wore a neat blue pin-striped suit, a starched white shirt, and a tartan plaid tie.

Often a comparison will be comprehensive, covering both similarities and dissimilarities, as in this passage:

> One cannot help but compare Viktor Frankl's approach to theory and therapy with the work of his predecessor, Sigmund Freud. Both physicians concern themselves primarily with the nature and cure of neuroses. Freud finds the root of these distressing disorders in the anxiety caused by conflicting and unconscious motives. Frankl distinguishes several forms of neurosis, and traces some of them (the noögenic neuroses) to the failure of the sufferer to find meaning and a sense of responsibility in his existence. Freud stresses frustration in the sexual life; Frankl, frustration in the *will-to-meaning*.[24]

h. Evaluation

Evaluation is judging the worth of something, often an idea or an approach. It involves critical examination of advantages and disadvantages, strengths and shortcomings of the thing judged. And it sometimes involves suggesting alternatives, as the author of this evaluation does:

[24] Gordon Allport, in Viktor Frankl, *Man's Search for Meaning* (New York: Simon & Schuster, Washington Square Press, Inc., 1963), pp. x-xi.

I doubt whether a doctor can answer this question [what is the "meaning of life?"] in general terms. For the meaning of life differs from man to man, from day to day and from hour to hour. What matters, therefore, is not the meaning of life in general but rather the specific meaning of a person's life at a given moment. To put the question in general terms would be comparable to the question posed to a chess champion, "Tell me, Master, what is the best move in the world?" There simply is no such thing as the best or even a good move apart from a particular situation in a game and the particular personality of one's opponent. The same holds for human existence. One should not search for an abstract meaning of life. Everyone has his own specific vocation or mission in life; everyone must carry out a concrete assignment that demands fulfillment. Therein he cannot be replaced, nor can his life be repeated. Thus, everyone's task is as unique as is his specific opportunity to implement it.

As each situation in life represents a challenge to man and presents a problem for him to solve, the question of the meaning of life may actually be reversed. Ultimately, man should not ask what the meaning of his life is, but rather must recognize that it is *he* who is asked. In a word, each man is questioned by life; and he can only answer to life by *answering for* his own life; to life he can only respond by being responsible. Thus, logotherapy sees in responsibleness the very essence of human existence.[25]

It is also useful to evaluate expressions commonly used in discussing controversial questions. Such evaluation can help us discover how full or empty of meaning the expressions are and, accordingly, how they serve to advance or retard communication.

Frequently in discussions of the question of obscenity someone will use the term "community standards" in a sentence like "That film surely violates community standards of decency." From all outward appearances the term is meaningful to speaker and listeners alike. Yet appearances can be deceiving, and it is appropriate to wonder how clear this term's meaning really is.

Should we understand "community standards" as a reference to *the* community or *a* community? If we say *the* community, people in general, the human family, immediately we realize that we are speaking of the inhabitants of Tokyo and Bremerhaven and Minsk and Lima, and that it is unlikely that the considerable cultural differences involved are compatible with the idea of one set of standards. We need a more homogeneous grouping: clearly we can settle only for *a* community. We can try the United States. What are the

[25] Viktor Frankl, *Man's Search for Meaning* (New York: Simon & Schuster, Washington Square Press, Inc., 1963), pp. 171-73. Reprinted by permission of the Beacon Press, copyright © 1959, 1962 by Viktor Frankl, and by Hodder and Stoughton Ltd.

"community standards" of decency in the United States? Here, too, we find difficulties since the standards in a small town will usually be more restrictive than those in a large city. And if we say small town standards are the "community standards" then we will not be reflecting city standards.

Perhaps the term is meaningful when used for the standards of a hypothetical "typical" hybrid of small town and big city—for example, a small city of about fifty thousand inhabitants representing a cross section of occupations, religious beliefs, educational and cultural backgrounds, and age groups—college professors, plumbers, doctors; Catholics, Protestants, Jews; and so on. What would the "community standards" be in this typical community? There would probably be less than perfect agreement. And even if there were widespread agreement about such matters as nudity in the shopping plaza, there would undoubtedly be much less agreement about nudity on the movie screen.

In short, the term "community standards" is far from being clear; it is obscure and serves effectively to block communication.

i. Prediction

Prediction is usually understood as loosely speculating what will happen in the future, flatly stating with pretense of authority that such and such will come true. That form of prediction is rightly rejected as unscholarly and of no value in writing directed to an intelligent audience. Obviously, that is not the sense in which the technique referred to here should be understood. Scholarly prediction involves speculating about the outcome of certain actual or potential conditions—that is, what may or might, can or could, probably will or should, happen. In other words, it offers an educated, logical guess on the basis of conditions known or hypothesized. It is used wherever it is necessary or desirable to project future effects of present actions. Here is an example of its use:

> The grave danger [in contemporary western civilization] is that, little by little, a whole generation will be drawn to believe that society is a conspiracy against it. The personal sense of having a place in the civilized state grows fainter; and if it collapses, the young become in fact and the old become in spirit members of those robber bands of homeless children which have now roamed Europe after two wars.[26]

26 J. Bronowski, *The Face of Violence* (New York: The World Publishing Company, 1967), p. 58.

j. Tracing and Summarizing

Technically these are not techniques for conducting or presenting the results of an analysis, but they are used with those techniques. Tracing is determining the line of growth or development of something—for example, the short story, American isolationism after World War I, trade unionism. It demands a coherent, but usually not a comprehensive or detailed, presentation of the origin and the significant stages of development of the subject. Its compactness makes it a very useful technique in situations where some historical background for an issue is needed, but space limitations demand brevity. Here is an example of tracing:

> As early as 1647, Margaret Brent demanded a "place and voyce" in the Maryland Assembly. Although she was the executrix of Gov. Leonard Calvert's will, her request was denied. From 1691 to 1780 women who were property owners voted in Massachusetts. After the Revolution, New Jersey temporarily granted suffrage to women when, in 1790, a revision of the electoral law used the words "he or she"; some women voted under this provision until 1807, when the legislature limited the vote to white male citizens.
>
> By the 1830s and 1840s increasing efforts were being made to awaken women to ask for full enfranchisement. . . . Books such as Margaret Fuller's *Woman in the Nineteenth Century* (1845) had an influence. Then, in June 1848, Elizabeth Cady Stanton, Lucretia Mott, Martha C. Wright, and Mary Ann McClintock issued a call for a convention to discuss the rights of women. Meeting in the Wesleyan chapel at Seneca Falls, N. Y., on July 19 and 20, the convention adopted a Declaration of Principles patterned on the American Declaration of Independence. Signed by 68 women and 32 men, the Seneca Falls declaration stated: "We hold these truths to be self-evident: that all men and women are created equal. . . ." [27]

Summarizing is briefly drawing together from a piece of our [28] writing all or selected assertions and presenting them in a compact, coherent passage without the evidence and analysis that support them. This technique is sometimes used at the end of a piece of writing. (Certain formats for scientific and technological writing call for such a summary at the beginning of the paper.) It can be

[27] *Encyclopedia Americana*, 1970 ed., S. V. "Woman Suffrage."
[28] Summarizing as it is used here does not include the handling of others' assertions. These and related subjects are discussed in *Techniques for Presenting Evidence*, item a, and in *Quoting*.

an aid to reading long pieces or shorter pieces that are highly complex or technical. However, unnecessary summarizing wastes the reader's time or insults his intelligence. In general, we should not summarize in most pieces of less than two thousand words.

11. Scope

Scope is the area covered by a piece of writing, the range of treatment. In some writing situations our purpose is to survey a broad area, not probing any part of it but limiting ourselves to a surface treatment. In virtually every subject articles and books of this type are written for the layman. However, when our purpose is to examine a difficult or controversial matter and to offer meaningful comment on it, we should prefer depth to breadth, probing analysis to skimming. To achieve such depth of treatment, we must limit the scope of our treatment to the number of aspects of our subject that we can handle effectively, and we do well in such cases to remember these words of Aldous Huxley:

> In practice we are generally forced to choose between an unduly brief exposition and no exposition at all. Abbreviation is a necessary evil and the abbreviator's business is to make the best of a job which, though intrinsically bad, is still better than nothing. He must learn to simplify, but not to the point of falsification. He must learn to concentrate upon the essentials of a situation, but without ignoring too many of reality's qualifying side issues. In this way he may be able to tell, not indeed the whole truth, for the whole truth about almost any important subject is incompatible with brevity, but considerably more than the dangerous quarter-truths and half-truths which have always been the current coin of thought.[29]

How can we be certain that the scope of a piece of writing is correct, that we have chosen neither too large nor too small an area to treat in the assigned length? Because of the great variety in writing situations, there is no specific formula to consult. But we may be confident that the scope is correct when we have achieved our purpose and met all the obligations that have arisen: to provide evidence, to explain or interpret, to analyze, and to fulfill certain responsibilities to our audience.

Closely related to the scope of the whole piece of writing is the

[29] *Brave New World Revisited* (New York: Harper & Row, Publishers, Perennial Library, 1958), pp. vii-viii.

scope of the assertions in it, the problem of degree of specificity. Most of us tend to generalize, particularly where our treatment of a subject is brief. We say "people in my neighborhood" or "the Irish" when we really have in mind "my next-door neighbor." There are, of course, valid and valuable generalizations to be made in even the briefest of writings. It would be wrong, therefore, to say the specific is inherently better than the general. Still, whenever we write, we should try to be as specific as is necessary to convey the point we are making.

12. Focus

In one sense, focus means the degree of clarity with which each idea in the piece of writing is presented. For example, if one of the assertions in a piece about dangers to human life is that the gasoline engine has been responsible for a large percentage of air pollution in the United States, we should not permit the evidence to blur the focus on the assertion as we present and interpret our evidence. In other words, if we are using statistics, we should not allow some detail to set us off on a tangential discussion of the nature of statistical processes or the range of activities of the particular research organization from which we have drawn our statistics.

In a larger sense, focus means the degree of clarity of the central idea in the piece. The central idea should be the dominant focus. Though there may be a number of secondary assertions and the evidence or analysis that supports or develops them may become the focus of one part of the piece, their relation to the central idea should be clear so that the larger, unifying idea retains its dominance. For example, the role of the gasoline engine in air pollution may be the focus of one part of the essay; the role of factories in air pollution may be the focus of another; assertions about types of water pollution, contamination of plant life by insecticides, and uncontrolled population growth may be the dominant ideas in other parts. And yet all these assertions may be subordinate to a central idea—that although scientific and technological advances have made human life safer and more comfortable, they have also threatened it, and if swift action is not taken at every level of government, this planet may well become uninhabitable.

Very few writers, including professionals, can get the exact focus they wish on the first draft. Even with the finest writers unintentional and undesirable shifting and blurring of focus can easily occur. And such errors can frequently be seen only after an entire rough draft has been completed. Therefore, the improvement of focus is one of the most important tasks to be accomplished in the process of revision.

13. Proportion

Proportion is the balance that exists when every matter taken up in a piece of writing is given the quality and amount of attention it deserves. Are primary concerns given primary emphasis? Does the treatment of secondary concerns reveal a reasonable ranking by relative importance? If the answers to these questions are affirmative, we say the piece of writing has proportion. If they are negative, we say it lacks proportion. If we were writing about a football game with the purpose of re-creating for the reader the excitement of the game's high points, we would not write paragraphs of equal length about the weather, the condition of the playing field, the first quarter action, the second quarter action, the half time show, the third quarter action, and so on. We would probably devote no more than a sentence or two to the weather and the condition of the playing field, omit the half time show altogether (no matter how interesting it may have been in itself), and skip quickly over the parts of the game that were relatively unexciting. We might very well devote half the paper to the final two minutes of play, if they were the most exciting minutes of the game.

Proportion is not determined so much by the nature of the subject as by the author's direct assertions or by the context he gives those assertions. For example, in an article about a current social issue, he can choose to focus exclusively on a very minor aspect of a single question. The only demand the concept of proportion would impose on him would be to distribute his attention reasonably—that is, to consider what details of the minor aspect are most significant and to give them the greatest attention. (To avoid misunderstanding in such cases, he should also *explicitly* acknowledge that the aspect is a minor one.)

Although this concept is a rather subtle one, it is really not difficult to observe. It is usually enough for us to remember to distribute the space in any piece of writing as nearly as possible according to the relative importance of what we are saying.

14. Quoting

Quoting another writer is not a sign of incompetency or lack of originality. It is rather a sign of maturity and responsibility, a mark of our ability and willingness to consult other thinkers and evaluate their knowledge and judgment about the subject. The mature writer does not accept others' judgments uncritically, it is true, but neither does he ignore them if they are relevant to his subject. When he agrees with a relevant judgment, he presents it *because* he agrees with it—that is, because it supports his own judgment. When he disagrees with it, he presents it *because* he disagrees with it, and wishes to offer the reader his criticism of it.

There are numerous ways to present a quotation. The most important consideration is to avoid awkwardness in doing so. Consider, for example, this quotation from John F. Kennedy:

> But when party and officeholder differ as to how the national interest is to be served, we must place first the responsibility we owe not to our party or even to our constituents but to our individual consciences.[30]

The writer who wishes to use this quotation in his composition may use one of three approaches: direct quotation, direct partial quotation, or indirect quotation. Note in each case how smoothly and naturally the previous material leads into the quotation.

Direct Quotation

(Note how the quotation marks are used when a comment by the writer interrupts the quotation.)

The public servant has many masters. But it is imperative that he decide which master deserves priority in which situation. Sometimes there is no conflict. "But," as John F. Kennedy wrote, "when party and officeholder differ as to how the national interest is to be served, we must place first the responsibility we owe not to our party or even to our constituents but to our individual consciences."

[30] *Profiles in Courage* (New York: Simon & Schuster, Inc., Pocket Books, 1957), p. 13.

Direct Partial Quotation

(Note the use of ellipsis, spaced periods to mark the omission of words. If the omission occurs at the beginning or in the middle of the quotation, three spaced periods are used; if at the end, four.)

The public servant has many masters. But it is imperative that he decide which master deserves priority in which situation. Sometimes there is no conflict. But when there is, in John F. Kennedy's view, "we must place first the responsibility we owe . . . to our individual consciences."

Indirect Quotation

(Note that in indirect quotation the wording of the quoted writer is not used and therefore no quotation marks are necessary. Note, too, how a reference to the work in which the quote appeared can be incorporated.)

The public servant has many masters. But it is imperative that he decide which master deserves priority in which situation. Sometimes there is no conflict. But I agree with John F. Kennedy's judgment in *Profiles in Courage* that when there is, the officeholder's personal conscience deserves the highest priority.

A direct quotation of more than ten lines would be set off in a separate paragraph and indented five spaces. It would be led into in the same manner as the examples above.

Although footnoting is the usual manner of crediting our sources, in a composition, as in a newspaper or magazine article, the mention of the quoted writer's name and the careful use of direct, direct partial, or indirect quotation is usually sufficient crediting. Reference to the work from which the quotation is taken is not necessary, though the thoughtful writer usually includes it, realizing that the reader may wish to read the quoted author's full development of the idea.

Which form of quotation we select depends on the relative quality of our source's expression. Whenever his wording is so clear, direct, vigorous, and concise that a paraphrase would be lengthier and less effective, we should use direct quotation. Whenever only part of the passage is so expressed or only part is relevant to the issue, we should use direct partial quotation. In most cases, for reasons of economy we will use indirect quotation.

A quotation we disagree with can serve effectively to illustrate a point of view we are criticizing and provide us with a focus for our observations. Consider this quotation:

Religion sets up the soul as a barrier between man and the animals and makes a similar distinction between the man who is saved and the man who is not. . . .[31]

A writer who disagreed with this quotation might handle it in this manner:

> In *The Twelve Seasons* Joseph Wood Krutch suggests that "religion sets up a barrier between man and the animals and makes a similar distinction between the man who is saved and the man who is not. . . ." To begin with, religion does not "set up" the soul as a "barrier" between man and brute—it *acknowledges* it as a *difference* between them. Mr. Krutch seems to confuse point of view with intention. Secondly, although few religions in the past appreciated the complexity of the human soul, and many did pretend omniscience in the matter of the salvation of men, at least one religion, Christianity, clearly admonished from the beginning to "judge not, lest you be judged."

One caution about quoting others is in order here. Just as quoting appropriately can enrich our writing, quoting indiscriminately can destroy it. We need not worry about quoting, as long as we avoid depending on quotations to provide the direction for our writing, and use them *with* and not *instead of* our own thoughts.

15. Title, Introduction, Conclusion

a. Title

A title serves to capture the reader's attention and arouse his curiosity. It should therefore be "eye-catching." Not, of course, either blatantly or dishonestly. We would not be pleased to pick up a magazine, flip through it and spot the title "SEX, SEX, SEX" and then on beginning to read the article, find that it concerned salmon spawning. So we should not attempt to perpetrate any such a hoax on our readers. The title should be related to the central idea and may also be broadly suggestive of our position. It should be brief and specific.

Sometimes title is confused with *topic*. Ten students in a class may write on the topic "courage." Courage would be the subject that these papers have in common. But no one of the papers would be entitled COURAGE, because *the title of each should distinguish*

[31] Joseph Wood Krutch, *The Twelve Seasons* (New York: William Sloane Associates, 1949), p. 186.

it from the others. One student might decide that the best title to cover his paper is THE COURAGE OF ED SMITH. Another might use COURAGE: REAL AND FALSE. A third, WHAT IS COURAGE? A fourth, COURAGE AND PACIFICISM. The rest might not even mention the word in their titles. The choice would reflect the particular idea (and perhaps technique) of the piece.

As a rule, the best time to title a piece of writing is when it is completed, because only then can we see what it says well enough to title it appropriately.

b. Introduction

An introduction serves to stimulate the reader's interest or, when the purpose is to persuade, to establish some basis of agreement with the reader or express our understanding of his position. It may also prepare him for the central assertion by narrowing the topic. For techniques that may be effective in introducing a paper, consult *Assertions, Techniques for Presenting Evidence,* and *Techniques of Analysis.* Some common introductory approaches are to ask a thought-provoking question, to present a significant fact or statistic, or to explain the importance of the problem the paper deals with.

In a short composition there is often no introduction—that is, the composition begins with the central assertion itself. If an introduction is used, it is important that it be natural. If we are forced to choose between an awkward or contrived introduction and none at all, we should not hesitate to choose the latter.

c. Conclusion

A conclusion serves to draw the composition together and, if possible, to reinforce the main assertion. It should *not* introduce a new aspect of the topic. For techniques that may be effective in concluding a piece, consult *Assertions, Techniques for Presenting Evidence,* and *Techniques of Analysis.* Some common approaches to concluding are to restate the central assertion or to summarize, bringing together a number of assertions made in various parts of the paper (neither of these approaches is effective in a short paper, as a rule); to quote a pertinent point, especially one made by an authority on the subject; or to suggest a course of action.

In a short composition there is often no conclusion—that is, the composition ends with the final point of evidence or analysis. It is most important that the conclusion not be "tacked on" but be the natural end of the composition.

ORGANIZATION

16. The Importance of Organization

To realize the importance of organization—the arrangement of the parts of the composition—we need only consider its relation to *meaning*. Organization and meaning are often inseparably intertwined; the order in which the parts of the composition occur is the order in which they register on the reader's mind, the precise impact of the first point influencing his reaction to the next. Organization is thus never an arbitrary concern; variations in organization create variations in meaning.

Moreover, if the organization is orderly and purposeful and if each new movement seems to the reader a reasonable progression from the previous one, the clarity of the writer's message is increased. In addition, as the reader progresses through the piece, the effective arrangement tends to increase his confidence in the writer —the writer's control over his writing subtly suggests his mastery of the subject he is writing about. The following excerpts illustrate this point. They are from a section of German historian Theodor Mommsen's famous work, *The Portrait of Julius Caesar*. With the exception of the final excerpt, they are the beginnings of a series of paragraphs; the final one is the end of the last paragraph in the series:

> The first ruler over the whole domain of Romano-Hellenic civilization, Gaius Julius Caesar, was in his fifty-sixth year (born 12 July 102 B.C.) when the battle at Thapsus, the last link in a long chain of momentous victories, placed the decision as to the future of the world in his hands. Few men have had their elasticity so thoroughly put to the proof as Caesar—the sole creative genius produced by Rome, and the last produced by the ancient world, which accordingly moved on in the path that he marked out for it until its sun went down. . . .
>
> If in a nature so harmoniously organized any one aspect of it may be singled out as characteristic, it is this—that he stood aloof from all ideology and everything fanciful. . . .

Caesar was thoroughly a realist and a man of sense; and whatever he undertook and achieved was pervaded and guided by the cool sobriety which constitutes the most marked peculiarity of his genius. . . .
Gifts such as these could not fail to produce a statesman. From early youth, accordingly, Caesar was a statesman in the deepest sense of the term, and his aim was the highest which man is allowed to propose to himself—the political, military, intellectual, and moral regeneration of his own deeply decayed nation, and of the still more deeply decayed Hellenic nation intimately akin to his own. . . .
The most remarkable peculiarity of his action as a statesman was its perfect harmony. . . .
He was monarch; but he never played the king. Even when absolute lord of Rome, he retained the deportment of the party-leader; perfectly pliant and smooth, easy and charming in his conversation, complaisant towards everyone, it seemed as if he wished to be nothing but the first among his peers. . . .
Such was this unique man, whom it seems so easy and yet is so infinitely difficult to describe. . . .
With reason therefore the delicate poetic tact of the nations has not troubled itself about the unpoetical Roman, and on the other hand has invested the son of Philip with all the golden luster of poetry, with all the rainbow hues of legend. But with equal reason the political life of the nations has during thousands of years again and again reverted to the lines which Caesar drew; and that fact, that the peoples to whom the world belongs still at the present day designate the highest of their monarchs by his name, conveys a warning deeply significant and, unhappily, fraught with shame.

This quality of purposeful arrangement we call *coherence*. It is found in all effective writing. Various ways to achieve coherence are the principal subject of sections seventeen through twenty-three, which follow.

17. Grouping vs. Separating

There are occasions when we should or must group a series of assertions rather than separate and develop them: for example, when our purpose in a piece of writing demands that we briefly trace a series of events or summarize someone's reasoning about our subject. But unless the occasion demands such a grouping, we should be careful to separate our assertions, developing each in turn. It is a common error, particularly among beginning writers, to attempt to say everything in their composition at once, in their haste often including matters that are outside the scope of the paper. Here is a fairly typical example of this error:

> (1) Some people believe that juvenile delinquents are sick and do not realize the difference between right and wrong. (2) I agree that some juvenile delinquents are "twisted" because of poor environment. (3) Delinquents living in slums have probably been exposed to crimes and delinquency all through their youth. (4) They have always seen crimes committed, so they commit them, not knowing the real difference between right and wrong because of their warped attitudes. (5) When they get caught by the police, the story is splashed in the newspapers and they are branded by society as outcasts. (6) This may be unjust. (7) But many delinquents are just plain hoodlums who roam in gangs. (8) Their crimes should be publicized. (9) The newspapers should print some of the good things that teenagers are doing for society, instead of only what the delinquents are doing.

The first six sentences all relate to the same subject, deprived youngsters who have turned to delinquency. Sentence six probably should be followed by an explanation of exactly why it is "unjust." The seventh sentence relates to a different subject and demands supporting evidence. The eighth sentence requires an explanation of why their crimes should be publicized. (The scope of the paper permitting, the two types of delinquency might be compared in some detail, using one or more of the techniques of analysis explained in section ten.) The final sentence is on a completely different topic, which would probably need an entire composition for adequate development. It should therefore be omitted from this composition.

18. Patterns of Organization

a. Time Order

In time order things are arranged according to their occurrence in time—what happened first is mentioned first, what happened second is mentioned second, and so on. Time order is most commonly used with brief or extended illustration. For example, "He arrived at the party at 10:30 and, after greeting everyone, motioned John to the balcony. They talked for almost an hour, seemingly in anger. Later . . . About 12:30 . . . Then . . ." It is also used in presenting a process and in comparing descriptions (or figurative definitions). In the latter case, the description of something "then" or "before" is followed by the description of it "now" or "later."

b. Space Order

In space order things are arranged according to their location in relation to some fixed point, usually the viewer's point of vision. Thus, the writer's order of discussion will reflect the order of distance (from far to near or near to far), the order of vertical direction (from higher to lower or lower to higher), or the order of horizontal direction (from left to right or right to left). Space order is most commonly used in description and in some presentations of process.

c. Inductive (Deductive) Order

In inductive order examples or details are presented first and then the conclusion that we draw from them. In deductive order the conclusion is presented first and then the examples or details that support it. Deductive order is more common than inductive, but in situations where the reader is likely to respond to the conclusion with disbelief or anger, inductive order is preferable.

d. Cause to Effect (Effect to Cause) Order

In cause to effect order a phenomenon is acknowledged and then its *effects* are identified. In effect to cause order a phenomenon is acknowledged and then its *cause* is identified. The demands of the writing situation govern which of these types of order should be used: if the question being asked is "what effect will this have?" we use cause to effect, if "what caused this to happen?" then effect to cause.

e. Order of Complexity

In this order the simpler aspects of a subject are dealt with first, then the more complex ones. The space devoted to the latter, of course, will be greater because the need for explanation is greater.

f. Order of Importance

In order of importance details or arguments are arranged in ascending order—the less important first, then the more important.

This order subtly suggests to the reader, as he progresses through the composition, that the writer's case is gaining strength. (The reverse order, more important to less important, is never used—except where the author's point is ironic or humorous—because it carries the suggestion that the writer's case is losing strength.) In addition, this order gives the writer the advantage of having his best argument presented last—in the position of greatest emphasis. What the reader reads last will usually remain clearest in his mind, and the impression he forms of it will largely govern his overall reaction.

In some writing situations, especially those dealing with controversial issues, we may wish to modify order of importance slightly and begin not with the least important detail or argument but with the *second most important*. This modification improves the chance not only that the reader's first reaction will be favorable, but also that his later reactions will tend to be, since first reactions influence later reactions.

19. Combining Patterns

In many writing situations the purpose and evidence will suggest the use of a single pattern of organization: reporting a noteworthy incident that happened on a college campus last week may require only a time pattern; stating our views on a proposed piece of legislation may require only order of importance. The single pattern is often found in very brief articles in journals of current events and opinion, even in articles (of limited scope) about highly complex issues. But in longer articles it is more common to find two or more patterns of organization used in combination, with one pattern dominating, as in these examples:

1. A psychiatrist's presentation of a single case history to illustrate the steps in the process of diagnosis. Inductive order dominates—the movement is from specific observations to overall diagnosis—but the observations are presented in time order.
2. An article presenting the writer's analysis of the causes of the increase in crime in the United States in recent years. The dominant order is effect to cause, but the causes are arranged in order of importance, or perhaps modified order of importance.

In books, though the combinations of patterns are more numerous, the structure is fundamentally the same—one pattern dominates the overall work and other patterns are employed to present the various evidence and analyses. For example:

1. In a western civilization textbook, time order will usually dominate—the section on the Middle Ages will be followed by the section on the Renaissance, which will be followed by the section on the Reformation. But within each section space order will be used (the Italian Renaissance will be developed in a different subsection from that of the English Renaissance); and within each subsection, cause to effect order or order of complexity or importance.

2. In an introductory philosophy textbook, order of complexity may dominate, with simpler concepts preceding more difficult ones. But within a section dealing with one particular concept, time order may be used to present various stages in the development of the concept, and space order to present different developments that occurred simultaneously in different places. Inductive or deductive order may be used to show how a philosopher's observation or speculation led him to take a particular philosophical position.

Thus, there is no single prescription for organizing, no one right pattern or combination of patterns. Different purposes in writing will create different obligations, and different evidence will suggest different possibilities. As a writer gains experience, much of the job of organizing becomes almost automatic. For the beginning writer, however, the job of organizing must be conscious. One of the simplest ways to decide which combination of patterns will be most effective is the following:

1. Consider the purpose of the composition; ask whether it suggests a pattern (perhaps the dominant one).
2. Consider the material to be presented and the technique of presenting it (illustration, definition, evaluation, etc.); ask whether it demands a particular pattern.
3. Determine the various ways the patterns in 2 can be combined with the one in 1.
4. Select the combination that you think would be most effective with your reader.

20.   Placement of the Central Assertion

The central assertion is often placed directly after the introduction, but it need not be. It may itself be the introduction or may be placed in the middle or at the end of the composition. Although if it is brief it is usually placed in a paragraph with other material, for emphasis it may be given a separate paragraph.

21. Transitions

Transitions are links between parts of the composition. The word "transition" is derived from the Latin *trans*, meaning "across," and *ire*, meaning "to go." A transition is therefore a going across, a bridge. It covers gaps in thought and provides the reader with the necessary signal to the desired reading of our expressions; it tells him how what we will say next relates to what we have already said. The skilled writer knows that it is not enough to say, "The reader will be able to figure out what I mean"; he knows he must make clear what he means. The uses of transition and some common examples of transitional expressions are as follows:

> When we are *adding* something to what we have said, we can show the relationship of what follows to what has gone before by using one of these expressions: *and, in addition, also, another example, secondly (thirdly, etc.).*
>
> When we are *intensifying*—that is, adding an even more significant thought or example, we may use *moreover, indeed.*
>
> When we are *contrasting,* taking up the other side of a question or presenting a contrary example, we may use *but, however, on the other hand, nevertheless.*
>
> When we are *concluding,* we may use *therefore, for this reason (these reasons), in conclusion, consequently.*
>
> When we are *indicating a change in time,* we may use *soon after, later that day (a year or two later, etc.), meanwhile.*

We may, of course, find it necessary to use a longer phrase, even a complete sentence or two, to bridge our thoughts adequately. Such a sentence is usually placed at the beginning of the new paragraph rather than at the end of the preceding one. Here are some examples of transitional sentences:

Transitional Sentence	Comment
Another example of my irrational fear, less serious than the first, but equally disturbing, occurred last week.	This signals that the writer is adding something to what he has said and reveals its relative importance.

Is today's scientific and technological knowledge sufficient to solve this problem?	This signals that the writer is turning from the problem itself to the question of man's capacity to deal with it.
The obstacles to be overcome in applying this theory are numerous.	This signals a move to the difficulties involved in applying the theory.

22. Paragraphing

Before the growth of the newspaper and magazine into mass media, writers generally used long paragraphs, some running to several book pages. But the advent of the newspaper and magazine brought column printing, which substituted a width of 1¾ inches for 5 to 8 inches, making even the shortest paragraph almost three times as long as it would be on a full-width page. This development, as well as the modern reader's disdain for formidable paragraphs, accounts for the modern writer's use of rather short paragraphs.

In addition to length, there are two other criteria for determining when to end one paragraph and begin another. One is the change from one technique to another. If we made three major moves in our composition—let us say from definition to comparison to reporting to evaluation—each move might suggest the start of a new paragraph. Another is a significant move within a technique: for example, from one point of comparison to another, or from one illustration to another. These criteria, however, are secondary to length. If the definition, comparison, reporting, and evaluation were all brief, they might be placed in one or two paragraphs rather than four. On the other hand, if a single definition or point of comparison were rather long, we might present it in two or more paragraphs.

Most magazines and journals generally prefer moderation in paragraphing—that is, paragraph length somewhere between the archaically long and the journalistically short, averaging perhaps between 75 and 150 words (somewhat longer in some professional and technical journals). One common exception to this general rule is the occasional use of a very short paragraph for emphasizing the central assertion or an especially important judgment. Another exception is the use of dialogue, in which a new paragraph is begun each time there is a change of speaker.

STYLE

23. Limitations of Language

Most of us recognize, sometimes acutely, our own personal limitations in using language. We grope for a word or fumble for the best sentence structure to express our idea. But many of us fail to appreciate the limitations of language itself. The popular ideas that language is fixed and stable and that words have meanings in themselves are false. Language, like humans, is constantly changing—when men become aware of certain realities, they create or adapt words to speak of them; when their interest in the realities passes, the words fall into disuse and die. And words have no meanings in themselves; they have meanings to people. In some ways the meaning of a particular word is the same to all people who speak the language and are familiar with the word. It would be a rare English-speaking person who did not know the common meaning of the word *cat*. But in other ways the meaning of a particular word differs considerably between people. At the mention of the word *cat* ten different people would probably form ten different images. The woman whose childhood pet was a thoroughbred angora would form a different image than would a man whose cats had been of the species "alley." The word *cliff* would likely have very different associations for a mountain climber, an artist specializing in seascapes, and a woman who fears heights.

Similarly, differences in awareness and understanding also affect the meanings we assign words. Most of us probably take the words *and, but, to,* and *for* for granted—that is, we use them without paying any attention to their different functions in different contexts. But to the linguistic philosopher they represent a world of complex meanings and problems.

Some words are necessarily indefinite. *Red* can be used to describe any one of a multitude of shades. *Tall is* a relative term: is a 5′ 11″ man tall? A three-story building? Abstract words have especially wide variations in meaning. What do *truth, justice,* and *faith* mean? Many things, with almost as many variations as there are people, and with constant modifications effected by discoveries in human knowledge and developments in human affairs. Not surprisingly, the words that we use most frequently in controversial issues are frequently the words whose meanings vary most widely —*poverty, foreign aid, population control, protest, power.*

Because of these limitations of language, as well as because of our personal limitations in using it, it is naive for us to expect any human communication to be perfect. The best we can hope for is to anticipate gaps in communication and overcome them by making our meaning as clear as possible to our readers or listeners and attempting to understand theirs. The rhetorical concepts included under the heading "Style" and presented in the remainder of this section help us to achieve these ends. Thus they are not special matters of interest only to the professional writer—the artist—but the basic elements of expression that every writer who wishes his words to be understood should master and observe.

24. Clarity

Clarity is the absence of ambiguity. Being clear means not settling for saying "roughly" what we intend, leaving the reader to figure out what we mean as best he can, but saying precisely what we intend. The very act of writing implies the obligation of the writer to eliminate, as effectively as he can, any gaps between his intended meaning and the meaning his reader is likely to receive. The following reminders can help us honor that obligation:

1. Unless you have a good reason to be vague or indefinite, be definite. A college instructor may make the vague statement, "Excessive absences from this class will be penalized" because he wishes more flexibility in dealing with students than he would have with a definite statement like "Anyone who has three absences from this class will be penalized one letter grade on his final grade." But if he does not have this reason or another good reason to be vague, he should be definite, since clarity would be better served by definiteness.

2. In dealing with abstract terms, relate them to concrete applications whenever possible. A discussion of "freedom" is more apt to be clear (and meaningful) if it occurs not in isolation but in a particular human context.

3. Be as specific as your intention suggests you should be. If you are writing about "Union soldiers in the Civil War," you should avoid referring to "soldiers in the Civil War," for the reader will think that you are referring to Confederate soldiers as well. Similarly, if you are making a comment about several students

in one of your classes, the reference "students in this college" will be too general.

25. Simplicity

"The language of truth," said Marcellinus Ammianus, fourth-century Roman historian, "is unadorned and always simple." And though it has been often honored in the breach in the more than two thousand years that have passed since it was made, that assertion remains an important principle of rhetoric. Real strength and dignity are found, not in clotted and convoluted, but in simple, direct, natural expression.

There are, of course, times when we can improve our writing by substituting a vigorous word for a mild one, a vividly concrete phrase for a lukewarm generalization. And times when we should recast whole paragraphs by combining a series of monotonously short sentences into a complex or compound sentence. These changes do not mean a loss of simplicity but a gain in force and variety. But we do lose simplicity if we make a single sentence more involved than need be, or if we require the reader to struggle unnecessarily to understand it.

We all enjoy the writing of someone whose expression is smooth and natural, who makes reading not a chore but a joy. And when we see another piece of writing by such an author, we are eager to read it. Who, for example, remembers the name of the main speaker at the dedication of a part of Gettysburg battlefield on November 19, 1863? His name was Edward Everett, a famous orator of that time. And he delivered a two-hour address. No one today remembers that long and probably eloquent address, but everyone remembers the brief talk of the man who, as an afterthought of the planners of the occasion, was asked to make "a few appropriate remarks" now known as "The Gettysburg Address." That memorable speech contains a total of 267 words. *And 194 of them are one syllable words.* (Fifty-three are two syllables and only twenty more than two syllables.) That is simplicity; and it is no coincidence that it is also greatness.

One obstacle to simplicity is *fine writing*, which is characterized by pretentiously ornate, often archaic diction. Beginning writers sometimes use it to move the reader to emotion; the reader's response is usually amusement or disgust.

Fine Writing	Simplicity
The susurrating field exuded the multitudinous olfactory delights of the vernal solstice.	The field murmured softly in the wind, smelling sweetly of spring.

A more formidable obstacle to simplicity is *jargon*, the special terminology used by those in a particular field. There is legal jargon, scientific jargon, and so on. But the term also refers to a common quality of such terminology and phrasing—unintelligibility. Here is how George Orwell believed the modern writer of jargon might have written a passage from *Ecclesiastes:* [32]

Jargon Version	Original
Objective consideration of contemporary phenomena compels the conclusion that success or failure in competitive activities exhibits no tendency to be commensurate with innate capacity, but that a considerable element of the unpredictable must invariably be taken into account.	I returned and saw under the sun, that the race is not to the swift, nor the battle to the strong, neither yet bread to the wise, nor yet riches to men of understanding, nor yet favour to men of skill; but time and chance happeneth to them all.

As this comparison reveals, jargon seems to be written for machines rather than for people. It never impresses the reader; it depresses him. Jargon cannot be eliminated from our writing by omitting some words; the entire passage in which it occurs must be rewritten. The best approach to such rewriting is to study the passage, decide what it is supposed to say, and then say it simply and directly. We can avoid using jargon inadvertently by consciously guarding against the following:

1. Most words ending in *-wise*. For example, *finance-wise, pleasure-wise, prestige-wise*. An exception is the useful word *otherwise*.
2. Any word ending in *-ize* for which there is an acceptable substitute. For example, *finalize (finish)* or *internalize (incorporate* or *assimilate)*. Some *-ize* words, of course, cannot be avoided— *materialize, recognize, summarize, organize*.
3. Unnecessarily big words for the context.
4. Inflated phrases. For example, *prior to* instead of *before*, *subsequent to* instead of *after*, *with respect to* instead of *about* or *in*, *due to the fact that* instead of *because*.

[32]*Politics and the English Language* (New York: Harcourt Brace Jovanovich, Inc., 1950).

26. Rhythm

Rhythm refers to the sound of writing, its effect upon the ear. Like good music, good writing should be melodious—that is, it should sing to the ear. This characteristic may seem a feeble one, hardly to be found in the strong, crisp writing that is characteristic of the Anglo-Saxon roots of our language. But the melodiousness I refer to is not incompatible with strength and crispness. Rather, it complements that type of writing by providing harmony within and among the sentences; it balances and gives greater force to blunt passages.

The skillful use of phrases and clauses is the principal way to achieve rhythm in writing. Consider the following passage from Robert Frost's writing. Read it aloud.

> A dramatic necessity goes deep into the nature of the sentence. Sentences are not different enough to hold the attention unless they are dramatic. No ingenuity of varying structure will do. All that can save them is the speaking tone of voice somehow entangled in the words and fastened to the page for the ear of the imagination. That is all that can save poetry from sing-song, all that can save prose from itself.

A very melodious passage. But what makes it so? If we were to answer the instinct or intuition a great writer like Frost has for his craft, we would be partly correct. For some people are born "gifted" in language. They have a particular talent, even genius, for speaking and writing. But there is another side to this truth. Effectiveness with language is not only an art but a skill. The techniques that the gifted writer employs instinctively, the less gifted writer can employ consciously. And in the above passage, as in all rhythmic passages, the techniques are clearly observable.

Note first of all the artful repetition. "A dramatic necessity" (first sentence) is reinforced by "dramatic" (second sentence). "All that can save them" (fourth sentence) is reinforced by "all that can save poetry" and "all that can save prose" (last sentence). Repetition of course can very easily be overdone, and when it is the effect is monotony. But when it is skillfully used to add rhythm (as it is here) instead of to pad, the effect is a harmonious linking of the sentences that sounds good and increases clarity.

And there is more at work in this passage to create rhythm. The fourth sentence has a lilting quality to it that derives mainly from the use of prepositional phrases in combination—"of voice," "in the words," "to the page," "for the ear," "of the imagination." Notice also the present participle "speaking" and the past participles "entangled" and "fastened."

In working to develop a more rhythmic style, avoid awkward phrasing.

Awkwardness is a lapse in sentence rhythm or unity that renders the thought unclear or, if the lapse is serious, obscure. It is usually caused by a hasty phrasing and failure to revise first drafts. For example, the following sentence appeared in a book review:

> The book actually is a study of the two men Auerbach worked for and their methods, Dave Freedman and Fred Allen.

As the sentence is constructed, Dave Freedman and Fred Allen are not men at all, but "methods." What the reviewer obviously meant to say, but probably tried to say too quickly, was this:

> The book actually is a study of the two men Auerbach worked for— Dave Freedman and Fred Allen—and of their methods.

Similarly, the student who wrote the following sentence had a thought, and a rather good one, in mind. But he proofread too quickly and uncritically (if at all).

> I feel that the present-day attitudes of many young people towards sex are not of low morals but rather of a questioning and confused nature.

The awkwardness of that sentence gives the reader the impression that the *idea* is somehow deficient. "It doesn't sound right;" he would say, "it's not well thought out." But his impression would be entirely different and he would realize the idea is at least worth considering, is perhaps a subtle truth, if the writer had taken the trouble to rephrase it like this:

> I feel that many young people today are not really sexually immoral, but confused.

Like jargon, awkwardness cannot be corrected by omitting words. The awkward passage must be completely rewritten. To be effective writers and present our ideas in the most favorable light, we must learn to look critically at our writing and refuse to settle for any but the clearest statement of our thoughts. One of the best ways to detect "bad" passages is to read aloud and listen for breaks in rhythm or unity.

27. Economy

Economy is a virtue in writing because the fewer the words, the less the reader's effort in grasping what we are saying. The less his effort, the less the possibility of confusion. In addition, economy is more forceful than wordiness.

To overcome wordiness in our writing, we need *not* (as with jargon and awkwardness) completely rephrase the passage. Usually we can achieve economy by omitting unnecessary words and slightly altering sentence structure. The most important principle here is the *principle of reduction*—whenever possible, reduce a sentence to a clause, a clause to a phrase, a phrase to a word. The following passage is essentially well-written, but it is wordy. By applying the principle of reduction we can increase its force.

> The doctor listened for the heartbeat that was not to be found. The doctor looked up and took a deep swallow. The doctor removed his stethoscope and covered the dead man with a blanket.

What immediately catches the reader's eye is the useless repetition of "the doctor," which results in an artificial breaking of the action into three sentences (This repetition could, however, be justified if the larger context demanded such an unusual emphasis.) Then too, "that was not to be found" announces what is clearly and dramatically implied in the last sentence. It interferes with the action. And "took a deep swallow" is more economically and no less effectively rendered "swallowed deeply." Note the improvement in the tightened version.

> The doctor listened for the heartbeat, looked, swallowed deeply, then removed his stethoscope and covered the dead man with a blanket.

The time to be concerned with wordiness is ordinarily not while writing the first draft but just before the final draft. And the way to proceed is to read through the entire piece looking for places where the principle of reduction can be applied without changing the meaning intended, to mark parts that need revision, and then to revise them one by one, deleting words and tightening the phrasing. Here are some examples of sentences so marked and the resulting revisions:

Wordy Passage	Revision
~~It was a figment of her imagination~~ that someone was staring at her.	She imagined that someone was staring at her.
The snow ~~was like a blanket that covered~~ the ground.	The snow blanketed the ground.
On the table Henry had placed a small object that ~~was the color of lavender.~~	On the table Henry had placed a small lavender object.
~~It seems to me that~~ he has ~~the desire~~ to improve his standing ~~in~~ class.	I think he wants to improve his class standing.
In the next booth ~~there~~ sat one of the best-known actors of our time.	In the next booth sat one of the best-known actors of our time.
After the conference ~~had concluded,~~ the committee chairmen met to share experiences.	After the conference, the committee chairmen met to share experiences.

28. Balance

One of the most effective ways to increase the coherence and force of a statement is to give it balance of form—that is, to make its various parts parallel to one another. Types of balance range from the simple pairing of two or more adjectives, nouns, verbs, or adverbs, to the more complex paralleling of phrases and clauses. Here are some examples:

Parallel Pairs

Adjectives	*Dirty and weary, alone and afraid,* the stranger wandered aimlessly through the forest.
Nouns	The real problems are not *violence and disorder,* but *apathy and irresponsibility.*
Adverbs	Joan studied *diligently and purposefully;* Edward, *sporadically and halfheartedly.*

Verbs	His world *was collapsing,* and he *was pursuing* a good time.

Parallel Phrases

Prepositional	This plan will benefit the students *of tomorrow* as much as the students *of today.*
Present Participial	He was ever at ease—whether *hunting lions in the African veldt* or *sipping wine with foreign diplomats.*
Past Participial	*His lips blistered, his throat parched, his eyes blinded* by the unrelenting glare of sun on sand, he staggered day after day across the merciless desert.
Gerund	*Dreaming of her, speaking about her, writing to her*—these activities filled his day and left no room for learning.

Parallel Clauses

Adjective	He is the one *who borrowed my money and never repaid it, who stole my notebook and blamed the theft on my roommate, who dated my girl and then laughed in my face.*
Noun	*That he dated my girl* is understandable; *that he laughed about it* is despicable.
Adverb	*Because he was honest,* he admitted his fear; *because he was courageous,* he overcame it.
	If you are too informal, he will regard you as impolite; *if too formal,* as snobbish.

As the second adverb clause indicates, the balanced sentence sometimes effects economy by permitting the omission of words that the sentence structure implies. Similarly, it affords greater control of the long sentence.

29. Variety

If all our sentences are about the same length and type, and begin in about the same way, their very sameness quickly lulls the reader into boredom and inattention. Monotony of style is the best guarantee that a writer will not be read. Therefore, if we wish to be read we must cultivate variety actively and consciously. Whenever we read our rough drafts, one of the first questions we should ask is, "Is my style varied enough to be interesting?" Consider this paragraph:

> The new student was mild by nature. He hated the very notion of violence. Therefore, he ignored the taunts of the school bully. He quietly accepted the verbal and even physical abuse. This was because a principle was involved. Yet when he heard his parents cursed, he became enraged. Then he turned on his tormentor. He pounded him unconscious.

This is clear enough. But it is dull, monotonous. There are too many sentences of the same length and structure. How can we change it? By studying the sentences to determine which can be effectively combined and then combining them, if possible using different types of sentences for each combination.

> Mild by nature, hating the very notion of violence, the new student ignored the taunts of the school bully. He quietly accepted the verbal and even physical abuse because a principle was involved. Nevertheless, when he heard his parents cursed, he became enraged, and turning on his tormentor, he pounded him unconscious.

This revision is more varied in sentence length and in structure. The first sentence is simple (one main clause with modifiers, no subordinate clauses). The second is complex (one main clause—"He quietly accepted . . ."—and one subordinate clause—"because a principle . . ."). The third is complex and compound (complex because it contains one main clause—"he became enraged . . ."—and one subordinate—"when he heard . . ."; and compound because of a second main clause—"he pounded him . . ."). It is also varied in sentence beginnings. Notice that the "he . . ." pattern is not so boringly repeated in the revision.

Notice how the even greater variety in the following passage makes it lively and interesting to read:

> In brief, the bass-voiced man of the chimney-corner was never recaptured. Some said that he went across the sea, others that he did not, but buried himself in the depths of a populous city. At any rate, the gentleman in cinder-gray never did his morning's work at Casterbridge, nor met anywhere at all, for business purposes, the

genial comrade with whom he had passed an hour of relaxation in the lonely house on the coomb.[33]

There are several relatively simple ways to increase variety in our writing:

To Vary Sentence Structure

1. Change two simple sentences into a compound sentence.

   Simple   We stayed at the dance for about an hour.
                  Then we went to Bill's house.

   Compound   We stayed at the dance for about an hour,
                  and then we went to Bill's house.

2. Change two simple sentences into a complex sentence.

   Simple   The firemen arrived. But the house had
                  already burned to the ground.

   Compound   When the firemen arrived, the house had
                  already burned to the ground.

The reverse changes can also be made, of course. If we find, for example, that a passage is monotonous because of too many *compound* or *complex* sentences, we can achieve variety by changing a few to *simple* sentences.

To Vary Sentence Length

1. Change one or two sentences from simple to compound or complex, or the reverse (as above).

2. Reduce a sentence or a clause to a *phrase* other than a participial phrase, and include it in another sentence, as was done in the passage revised at the beginning of this section.
   The new student was mild by nature. He hated the very notion of violence. Therefore, he ignored the taunts of the school bully.

---

[33] Thomas Hardy, "The Three Strangers," *Wessex Tales* (New York: Harper & Row, Publishers).

became

> Mild by nature, etc. (The first sentence was reduced to a phrase.)

3. Change a sentence or a clause to a *participial phrase,* and include it in another sentence, as shown in the passage revised in the beginning of this section.

> He hated the very notion of violence.

became

> *Hating* the very notion of violence, etc.

and

> Then he turned on his tormentor.

became

> *Turning* on his tormentor, etc.

The above changes were to *present* participles (*-ing*). (Where the sense of the sentence requires, we may also change to *past* participles (*-ed*).

> A man entered the room. He had a deep tan and was rather muscular.

becomes

> A deeply *tanned,* well-*muscled* man entered the room.

4. Change a clausal construction to a gerundive or an infinitive construction.

> When one takes a friend for granted, he jeopardizes their friendship.

becomes

> Taking a friend for granted is jeopardizing a friendship.

or

> To take a friend for granted is to jeopardize a friendship.

5. Take an appositive from a sentence and let it stand alone as a separate sentence. Such use, of course, constitutes a fragment. But this type of fragment is acceptable if not overused.

> Many girls go to college with one thought, marriage.

becomes

> Many girls go to college with one thought. Marriage.

To Vary Sentence Beginnings

1. Use a word out of its usual order.

   I *often* wonder what I'll do after I graduate from college.

   becomes

   Often I wonder what I'll do after I graduate from college.

2. Use a phrase out of its usual order.

   Jack caused the accident by failing to signal.

   becomes

   By failing to signal, Jack caused the accident.

3. Change the order of the clauses in a complex sentence.

   I expected to change my attitude toward studying when I came to college.

   becomes

   When I came to college, I expected to change my attitude toward studying.

There is one important qualification to be made about the above suggestions. We should never alter the structure or order of a sentence or paragraph to achieve variety at the expense of the precise expression of our idea. The question, "How can I gain greater variety in my expression?" should never take precedence over the more important question, "What do I wish to say?"

30. Emphasis

Emphasis means force, stress, prominence. A part of a sentence is said to have emphasis if it stands out from the other parts. A particular sentence is said to have emphasis if it stands out from a group of sentences. One of the easiest and most effective ways to gain emphasis is to *place a very short sentence after a series of comparatively long ones.* Often this involves rephrasing a passage, making a number of average-length sentences into two or three longer sentences and following them with a short sentence that contains the point we want to emphasize. In the following paragraph, for example, the sentences are all nearly the same length. The last sentence is not different enough to be really effective.

Somewhere in Russia a man attends classes faithfully. He does his homework diligently. He retains every detail of his subject perfectly. One could not tell him from any other Russian student in looks, manner, or dress. But he is different in one important respect. He is a future spy.

Now note how the last sentence is given greater force by combining the first five into two.

Somewhere in Russia a man attends classes faithfully, does his homework diligently, retains every detail of his subject perfectly. Although one could not tell him from any other Russian student in looks, manner, or dress, he is different in one important respect. He is a future spy.

Another way to create emphasis is to *repeat words skillfully. Skillfully* in this case means judiciously limiting the repetition to those sentences we wish to have the greatest force. It does not mean indiscriminate repetition, which is wholly ineffective. Note how in the following paragraph the word *power* is skillfully repeated:

He has the power to enter and to become what he sees and paints. It is a power bequeathed to him by his childhood, a power common to most children, but one lost away from them when they take that long change toward the physical and material life of adults. It is the power not so much to recognize what is there to be seen, but even while gazing at it to imagine it as if it had never before existed: a power without end to rediscover life continuously.[34]

Still another way to create emphasis is to *substitute a periodic sentence for a loose sentence.* A loose sentence is a complex sentence in which the main idea (main clause) is completed near the beginning. As the sentence continues it wears down, dissipating its strength. A periodic sentence, on the other hand, is a complex sentence in which the main idea (main clause) is completed at the end. The reader is less likely to lose interest and attention while reading it because it builds toward its main point.

Loose   We went out for a snack, although we knew we should have stayed at the meeting.

[34] Paul Horgan, "Andrew Wyeth," *Ramparts*, Christmas, 1963, p. 34.

Periodic	Although we knew we should have stayed at the meeting, we went out for a snack.
Loose	He refused to steal the car, despite the taunts of the rest of the gang and the threat of a beating he knew very well would be vicious.
Periodic	Despite the taunts of the rest of the gang and the threat of a beating he knew very well would be vicious, he refused to steal the car.

Naturally not all the sentences in a composition can be complex. In fact, in contemporary writing relatively few are; most are simple or compound. So the choice between periodic and loose occurs relatively infrequently. When it does occur we should remember that the sentences that should be periodic are those in which a clear reading of the qualifications we make on an idea is especially desirable, or which we want to be as dramatic and forceful as possible.

(See section 28 for an additional way to achieve emphasis.)

31. *Exactness*

Exactness means using the word that will convey our intended meaning most precisely—the word that has the denotation, the connotation, and the degree of specificity we wish.

a) Denotation is direct, literal meaning. No two words have exactly the same meanings. Many words have similar meanings. For example, *unbelief* and *disbelief* both signify not believing; but *unbelief* refers to simple absence of belief, and *disbelief* to *refusal* to believe. Words that have almost identical meanings we are apt to use interchangeably:

I was *conscious* of the hostility between them.

I was *aware* of the hostility between them.

I was *cognizant* of the hostility between them.

The denotative meanings of these words may seem exactly the same, yet *conscious* refers to an inner realization, *aware* to sensory realization, and *cognizant* to reasoning about sensory realization.

b) Connotation is implied or associative meaning, the favorable or unfavorable attitude that accompanies denotation. Some words are relatively neutral in connotation—there is no significant connotative difference among *conscious, aware,* and *cognizant,* for example. Others have very strong connotative meaning. Consider the following:

> He *managed* their books expertly.
>
> He *manipulated* their books expertly.

Both words have the general denotation of *handled* or *took care of.* But *managed* is relatively neutral and *manipulate* implies *deviousness.* Similarly, to call Senator Schultz a *politician* is quite different from calling him a *statesman,* for *politician* implies that his devotion to high principles is less than consuming. Because the connotations of our words can alter the meaning of what we say, we should choose our words carefully.

c) Degree of specificity refers to how closely we identify a person, thing, or state. At times we may wish to be very general, at other times, very specific. Since the degree of specificity can change from sentence to sentence and paragraph to paragraph, we should ask ourselves as we are writing, "How specific should I be in order for the reader to grasp my intended meaning?" Here are several examples of variations in specificity.

people ⎱
men ⎰   GENERAL

Two Marines entered the lounge.

Marine officers ⎱
Marine Captains ⎰   SPECIFIC

moved (GENERAL)

The tall man walked across the room.

lurched (SPECIFIC)

several things (GENERAL)

He left some books and papers on his desk.

two books, a manuscript and a letter (SPECIFIC)

sounds (GENERAL)

The night was filled with the sounds of dogs, gulls, the surf.

the howling of dogs, the flapping of gulls, the slow, rhythmic roar of the sea (SPECIFIC)

32. Vitality

Vitality is liveliness. In terms of writing it is the opposite of dullness, monotonousness, lifelessness. It is achieved principally in four ways:

a) By purging our writing of bland expressions—"It was a *great* game," "They're *nice* people," "It's a *good* film." Such expressions are crutches for those who do not want to think about what they're saying and choose their words accurately. The problem is that bland expressions can mean almost anything—and for that reason they are virtually meaningless. "Nice," for example, in the sentence above can mean (among other possibilities) "courteous," "agreeable," "attractive," "refined," "respectable," "friendly," "cultured."

b) By avoiding euphemisms—that is, indirect or vague expressions chosen because of fear that bluntness will be offensive. To say "he became ill" when we mean "he vomited" or "she passed away" when we mean "she died" or "John was indisposed" when we mean "John was roaring drunk" weakens our writing. There is such a thing as too-blunt writing—we can be offensive—but more often than not bluntness is a virtue. Slang and even profanity also have their place in writing, though they should be approached more judiciously because of the possibility that they will distract the reader. Still, when it seems natural to use them, we shouldn't hesitate to do so.

c) By using vivid verbs, adjectives, and adverbs, those that evoke sensory reactions in the reader. Consider, for example, this passage by George Orwell:

> When I pulled the trigger I did not hear the bang or feel the kick— one never does when a shot goes home—but I heard the devilish roar of glee that went up from the crowd. In that instant, in too short a time, one would have thought, even for the bullet to get there, a mysterious, terrible change had come over the elephant. He neither stirred nor fell, but every line of his body had altered. He looked suddenly stricken, shrunken, immensely old, as though the frightened impact of the bullet had paralysed him without knocking him down. At last, after what seemed a long time—it might have been five seconds, I dare say—he sagged flabbily to his knees. His mouth slobbered. An enormous senility seemed to have settled upon him. One could have imagined him thousands of years old. I fired again into the same spot. At the second shot he did not collapse but climbed with desperate slowness to his feet and stood weakly

upright, with legs sagging and head drooping. I fired a third time. That was the shot that did for him. You could see the agony of it jolt his whole body and knock the last remnant of strength from his legs. But in falling he seemed for a moment to rise, for as his hind legs collapsed beneath him he seemed to tower upward like a huge rock toppling, his trunk reaching skywards like a tree. He trumpeted, for the first and only time. And then down he came, his belly toward me, with a crash that seemed to shake the ground even where I lay.[35]

d) By using similes and metaphors. Simile is the direct comparison of two unlike things using "like" or "as." For example, "They stood listening attentively to the speaker's clichés and slogans, like a herd of cattle grazing on the grass that fattens them for the kill." Metaphor is the direct comparison of two unlike things without using "like" or "as." For example, "His aloofness was a wall of stone, at once keeping his thoughts and hopes and dreams in, and others' friendship out."

e) By choosing active rather than passive voice whenever possible. Active voice preserves the natural order of action—"Henry hit the ball hard." Passive voice inverts that order—"The ball was hit hard by Henry." There are occasions when we may wish to put the stress on that which was acted upon. Then we should use passive voice. But such occasions will be rare. We may, for example, say "I have been cheated by my roommate" if we want to stress that we have been wronged. But ordinarily we would use the stronger, more direct, "My roommate has cheated me."

33. Minor Stylistic Devices

a) A series of questions, appropriately placed, will heighten the reader's interest in our idea. For example, in the following passage the questions are not a necessary part of the development but are added to emphasize the importance and relevance of what follows them.

All colonial empires are in reality founded upon that fact. The people have brown faces—besides, there are so many of them. Are they really the same flesh as yourself? Do they even have names? Or are

[35] From "Shooting an Elephant" in *Shooting an Elephant and Other Essays* by George Orwell, copyright, 1945, 1946, 1949, 1950, by Sonia Brownell Orwell. Reprinted by permission of Harcourt Brace Jovanovich, Inc., and Secker & Warburg, Ltd.

they merely a kind of undifferentiated brown stuff, about as individual as bees or coral insects? They rise out of the earth, they sweat and starve for a few years, and then sink back into the nameless mounds of the graveyard and nobody notices that they are gone.[36]

b) By stating what we do not mean (or what is not the point) we can effectively prepare our reader to consider with heightened interest and fuller understanding what we do mean (or what is the point). This is called the "not that, but this" device.

The main problem of American college students today is not the largeness of colleges. Nor is it crowded living conditions, nor the arbitrariness of faculties and administrations. It is rather that they have never learned, and have never been taught, how to think.

c) We can very economically sum up our reaction to an idea or incident and provide a forceful beginning for the explanation of our reaction by using an exclamation. Note the effect of "A shocking statement!" in the following example.

A student recently told me that the most important problem on this campus in the view of students is the restrictive "cut" policy. A shocking statement! Shocking because (assuming it is true that students think this way) it reveals a concern for the trivial and a neglect of the crucial. Every campus has real, substantive issues touching the very core of education that demand the attention of faculty and students. And this campus is no exception. Yet these problems will remain unsolved unless we have the good sense to distinquish them from narrow, pedestrian concerns.

d) By reversing a phrase, we can often catch a subtlety of meaning too difficult to suggest otherwise, as did Winston Churchill in a speech at the Lord Mayor's Day Luncheon, November 12, 1942. (Note also the "not that, but this" pattern.)

Now this is not the end. It is not even the beginning of the end. But it is, perhaps, the end of the beginning.

e) The use of the "for" construction ("for" in the sense of "because") gives added force to an expression of the reasons we think as we do, as it does in this passage from Aristotle.

[36] George Orwell, "Marrakech," *Shooting an Elephant and Other Essays* (New York: Harcourt Brace Jovanovich, Inc., 1950).

Poetry is finer and more philosophical than history; for poetry expresses the universal, and history only the particular.

f) Beginning a sentence with a coordinating conjunction—*and, but, or, nor, for*—was for a time considered by some writing teachers to be bad form. Nevertheless, effective writers, from the anonymous author of the old English epic *Beowulf* to the most respected modern essayists and journalists have not hesitated to ignore this arbitrary rule. For they have recognized that these words are the clearest, most economical transitions in the English language.

g) For a time, sentence fragments were also regarded, without exception, as bad form. But modern writers use them freely to achieve greater emphasis and variety. Most modern writers do, however, avoid ineffective fragments—those that are too closely related to another sentence to stand alone.

Effective	Most students in this college are interested in just one thing. A good time.
Effective	We were all in a carefree mood. Except John.
Effective	As soon as we realized a riot was in the making, we left. And fast.
Ineffective	The boy jumped into the pool after his sister. Even though he couldn't swim. ("The boy jumped into the pool after his sister even though he couldn't swim" is better. The fragment is too dependent on the main clause to stand alone without being awkward. Further, it does not add significant emphasis or variety.)
Ineffective	Seldon and Willard were the last ones to leave the pool hall. Since their match was scheduled last. (As in the example above, one sentence would be smoother.)

h) Whenever we are enumerating points, we can increase their impact by proceeding from the least important to the most important. This device is called "order of climax."

> I hate war as only a soldier who has lived it can, only as one who has seen its brutality, its futility, its *stupidity*.
>
> Dwight D. Eisenhower

i) We can add stress to a key thought in a composition by expanding on it—that is, by presenting it and then repeating it in one or two different ways. This device is especially effective if the predicate is withheld until the end of the sentence, as in the periodic sentence.

> To die at the height of a man's career, the highest moment of his effort here in this world, universally honored and admired, to die while great issues are still commanding the whole of his interest, to be taken from us at a moment when he could already see ultimate success in view—is not the most unenviable of fates.[37]
>
> Winston Churchill

34. Punctuation

The only reason we use punctuation when we write is to make our expression clear to the reader. Without punctuation, writing would be unintelligible. It would make the reader falter and force him to reread almost every line. Consider, for example, the obscurity of the following passage when it is unpunctuated:

> For literary judgment we need to be acutely aware of two things at once of what we like and of what we ought to like few people are honest enough to know either the first means knowing what we really feel very few know that the second involves understanding our shortcomings for we do not really know what we ought to like unless we also know why we ought to like it which involves knowing why we don't yet like it it is not enough to understand what we ought to be unless we know what we are and we do not understand what we are unless we know what we ought to be the two forms of self-consciousness knowing what we are and what we ought to be must go together.

We don't have to read far into such a passage to get the feeling we are in an uncharted jungle of words—without a map. It is, of course, possible for us to figure out what the passage says but only after careful analysis and many false starts. If we had to approach everything we read in this time-consuming way, reading would be sheer torture. How much faster can we read that paragraph as T. S. Eliot really wrote it—that is, with punctuation?

> For literary judgment we need to be acutely aware of two things at once: of "what we like," and of "what we *ought* to like." Few people are honest enough to know either. The first means knowing what

[37] *Report on the War Situation,* House of Commons, December, 1940.

we really feel: very few know that. The second involves understanding our shortcomings; for we do not really know what we
ought to like unless we also know why we ought to like it, which
involves knowing why we don't yet like it. It is not enough to understand what we ought to be, unless we know what we are; and we
do not understand what we are, unless we know what we ought to
be. The two forms of self-consciousness, knowing what we are and
what we ought to be, must go together.[38]

It is not an easy passage in either case. It expresses some subtle
relationships that we must read carefully to comprehend fully. And
that is just the point. This example reveals not only the need for
careful punctuation in writing, but also the fallacy of the idea that
professional writers, especially great writers, can ignore with im-
punity the convention of punctuation. They cannot—not if they
seriously want to communicate. Nor can we.

Punctuation is not an arbitrary requirement of form, though it
can degenerate into that. It is not the maliciously imposed whim
of English teachers, though some English teachers act as if it were.
Punctuation is a device for increasing the effectiveness of one's
writing, a rhetorical device.

Punctuation marks are not, however, entirely a matter of free
choice. They are very much like traffic signs, which all give signals,
but differ in exactly what they signal. "Yield right of way" means
something quite different from "Stop." Punctuation marks are used
to signal subtle and even intricate matters, called by grammarians
stress (the degree of loudness in pronunciation), *pitch* (variations
in the vibrations of voiced sounds), and *juncture* (sound features
that appear at the points between words). To develop a complete
conceptual foundation for punctuation, it is necessary to study these
matters very closely. Perhaps you will wish to do so on your own.
However, space does not permit presenting here more than a simplified approach to punctuation. The basic distinction in punctuating
is the distinction between a *significant pause* and a *full stop*. A significant or breathing pause is marked by a comma, and a full stop
by a period, question mark, exclamation point, semicolon, colon, or
dash. An insignificant or non-breathing pause, which at one time
was also marked by a comma, is today left unmarked. The modern
writer prefers as few punctuation marks as possible, just as he
prefers as few words as possible.

Some high school English courses present a large number of rules

[38] T. S. Eliot, "Religion and Literature," *Essays Ancient and Modern* (New
York: Harcourt Brace Jovanovich, Inc., 1936).

for punctuation. Relatively few will be presented here. This omission does not mean that all the other rules are not valid. It means only that it is simpler and no less effective to understand the basic distinction between the pause and stop and the various ways of marking each, and then to *determine how to punctuate a particular passage by hearing the natural pauses and stops.* Teachers have found many reasons to conclude that knowing the rules of punctuation does not guarantee effective punctuation, and that not knowing them does not necessarily result in ineffective punctuation.

Marking Pauses

The *comma* is used to mark significant pauses. Such pauses occur in five common forms of expression:

Between Two Clauses	The sky was clear when we left on the hike, but before we had gone a mile it began to pour.
	Although they both had invitations to the party, only John went.
Between Words, Phrases, or Clauses in a Series	Miniskirts, go-go boots, stringy hair, dangling earrings, and dime-store jewelry are fashionable among hippies. (Pauses between words in a series)
	Stealing car accessories, shoplifting, and looting burned-out buildings are among the most prevalent forms of juvenile crime. (Pauses between phrases in a series.)
	The student who sets up and follows a realistic study schedule, who takes clear and comprehensive notes in his classes, and who completes his assignments on time is the student who is most likely to succeed in college. (Pauses between clauses in a series.)
After an Introductory Transition	However, he was one of the offenders.
	Therefore, I move that we adjourn.
Between Day of the Month and Year, City and State or Country	I was born January 3, 1920. My home is in Vienna, Austria.

Marking Stops

The *period* is the usual stop mark. (The use of the question mark needs no explanation. The exclamation point is used in place of the period to increase emphasis.) But we may use the *semicolon* in place of the period if we wish to show that the thoughts are closely related to each other.

Right   John arrived late. His brother never came at all.

or

Right   John arrived late; his brother never came at all.

Either mark would be acceptable here because the two sentences bear closely on one another. There is also another possibility: to *change the full stop to a pause* by joining the clauses with a conjunction—*and, but, or, nor, for,*—the choice depending on the sense of the passage.

Right   John arrived late, but his brother never came at all.

However, it would be wrong to join those two sentences with *just* a comma—that is, *without* changing the full stop to a pause.

Wrong   John arrived late, his brother never came at all.

The *dash* and *colon* also mark full stops. They may be used in place of the period to show that the words that follow the full stop identify or clarify those that precede it. (Note: in typing, the dash is made with two unspaced hyphens.)

There is one thing that college students have very little of—free time.

or

There is one thing that college students have very little of: free time.

The above example identifies the words that precede it. The following example does not identify—it clarifies.

My roommate is not too considerate—he keeps his pet gorilla in my closet.

or

My roommate is not too considerate: he keeps his pet gorilla in my closet.

Varying Emphasis

As was pointed out above, an interrupting or parenthetical statement is usually treated as a pause and set off by commas. This treatment neutralizes the interruption, gives it no more and no less emphasis than the rest of the sentence. If, however, we wish to give it more or less emphasis we may vary the punctuation.

Commas to *neutralize* it:

Two members of our team, John and Bill, received awards.

Dashes to *emphasize* it:

Two members of our team—John and Bill—received awards.

Parentheses to *de-emphasize* it:

Two members of our team (John and Bill) received awards.

Other Punctuation Marks: The Apostrophe

One use of the apostrophe is to mark the omission of letters in contractions—*didn't, can't, shouldn't it's, they're.* (Be sure to place it where the letters have been omitted.)

Another use is to indicate possession. The rule for using the apostrophe in this way is quite simple. *If the word ends in s just add the apostrophe; if it does not end in s, add both the apostrophe and* s. For example:

If we are referring to the coat that belongs to one boy, since *boy* does not end in *s,* we add both the apostrophe and *s*—that is, we say "the boy's coat."

However, if we are referring to the coats that belong to two or more boys, since *boys* ends in *s,* we add only the apostrophe —that is, we say "the boys' coats."

Similarly, the shoes of one child would be "the child's shoes"; the shoes of several children, "the children's shoes"; the home of Charles, "Charles' home."

Possession, of course, may concern not only personal belongings or property, but also qualities, characteristics, moods, reactions, and so on. It would therefore be appropriate to speak of "the plumber's patience," "my son's impetuousness," "a delinquent's hostility," "Mary's insulting remark," "Julius' sharp reply." [39]

[39] Until recently, correct usage demanded an additional *s* for words ending in *s*. Thus "Julius' sharp reply" would have been written "Julius's sharp reply." Since the modern form is simpler and does not cause any misreading of the possessive, many writers no longer observe the older form.

Note that the apostrophe is *not* used for possessive personal pronouns—*mine, yours, hers, its, ours, theirs*—or for the possessive relative pronoun *whose,* since the form of these words itself denotes possession.

Ellipsis

Ellipsis is the use of three spaced periods to mark the omission of one or more words in quoted matter. For example, we might wish to quote part of this passage from Thoreau:

> The mass of men serve the state thus, not as men mainly, but as machines, with their bodies. They are the standing army, and the militia, jailers, constables, posse comitatus, etc. In most cases there is no free exercise whatever of the judgment or of the moral sense; but they put themselves on a level with wood and earth and stones; and wooden men can perhaps be manufactured that will serve the purpose as well. Such command no more respect than men of straw or a lump of dirt. They have the same sort of worth only as horses and dogs. Yet such as these even are commonly esteemed good citizens.[40]

In our composition the passage might appear like this:

> The mass of men serve the state . . . as machines, with their bodies. They are the standing army, and the militia, jailers, constables. . . . In most cases there is no free exercise whatever of the judgment or of the moral sense. . . .

Note that the second and third omissions are marked with *four* spaced periods. The extra period indicates that the omission covers the end of the sentence. At times, we may even have to omit an entire paragraph or more from a lengthy quotation. (Lengthy quotations, of course, are seldom used even in lengthy pieces and never in brief ones.) This we mark by a *separate entire line* of spaced periods.

Whenever we use ellipsis, we should remember to check carefully, to be sure we have omitted no words necessary to preserve the author's meaning.

[40] Henry David Thoreau, "On The Duty of Civil Disobedience," *Aesthetic Papers,* ed. by Elizabeth Peabody, 1849.

Quotation Marks

Quotation marks are used before the first and after the last words of direct quotations:

"Give me liberty or give me death," Patrick Henry said.

Note that when the quotation does not end the sentence, and proper reading of the sentence demands a comma, the comma is placed within the quotes. If it does end a declarative sentence, the period is always placed within the quotes.

Patrick Henry said, "Give me liberty or give me death."

In addition to the placement of the period within the quotes, note also the placement of the introductory comma outside the quotes.

A question mark (or exclamation point) is always placed *outside* the quotes unless the punctuation itself is a part of the quotation.

Who said, "Give me liberty or give me death"?

but

The first thing he said was, "May I borrow a dollar?"

Similarly, semicolons, colons, and dashes are always placed outside the quotation marks unless they are part of the quotation.

Whenever we are quoting more than ten lines we should indent the entire quotation five spaces and *omit the quotation marks.* Occasionally, however, we may be using a format that does not allow for such indentation (for example a newspaper article). In such cases, when we are quoting more than a single paragraph, we should use quotation marks at the beginning of each paragraph and at the end of the final paragraph, but not at the end of the other paragraphs.

The title of a short story, a poem, a magazine article, or the chapter of a book is placed in quotation marks if we are *referring* to it; that is, if it was written by someone else, or if it was written by us at some prior time. The common practice of using quotes with our own titles (or underlining them) at the time we are writing them is incorrect.

Quotation marks are also used to indicate that an expression is itself the subject of discussion—"When we speak of 'spiritual matters,' we mean something quite different from what the medieval peasant, or even the medieval scholar, meant"; or to suggest that the appropriateness or validity of the expression is questionable— "We hear a great deal today about the 'new' morality." They should *not* be used with words that, though recently coined, have settled into the language—"hippies"; or as a device for sarcasm—"The 'food' in this 'college' is indescribable"—at least unless we are certain we can control it.

Underlining

Underlining in writing and typing is the equivalent of italics in printing. It is used principally for *emphasis*. But it is also used for foreign words, titles of books, plays, films, paintings and sculpture, magazines, newspapers, and the names of particular trains, planes, and ships.

Emphasis	I said to do it *now*. (To be effective this device must be used sparingly.)
Foreign Words	Israeli occupation of Jerusalem was once a dream. Now it is a *fait accompli*.
Title of a Book	William Stringfellow's *My People Is The Enemy* is very lucidly written.
Title of a Play	The play that impressed me most in high school was *Our Town*.
Title of a Film	*Citizen Kane* is a film classic.
Name of a Painting or Sculpture	*The Mona Lisa* is my favorite painting; *The Thinker*, my favorite sculpture.
Title of a Magazine	I read the *Saturday Review* every week.
Title of a Newspaper	The *New York Times* is my primary news source.
Name of a Ship	My cousin once sailed on the *Queen Mary*.

The common practice of underlining composition titles is incorrect.

Let me summarize the above principles of punctuation. The writer is not free to mark a full stop as a pause or a pause as a full stop. But he is free to *change* a pause into a full stop or choose the type of full stop that gives his words the desired reading. And he must consider the relationships among sentences. For this reason *punctuation should be selected for the entire paragraph rather than for each sentence by itself.* In most cases a paragraph can be punctuated in more than a single way. Different ways produce different emphases, which can increase the force and vigor of the composition if they are chosen carefully.

Consider, for example, the number of possibilities for punctuating the following paragraph, in which the writer chose to make his sentences rather short, probably because he was originally writing for a mass newspaper audience. The last three sentences create a hammer-like effect: quick, short strokes.

> Conscience, as the word indicates, is consciousness. It is a specific kind of consciousness—moral awareness, an inner sense of right and wrong. And it is an awareness that has compelling power. We feel bound by it. It commands us. If we disobey it, we feel remorse or anxiety.[41]

Had he been writing solely for college graduates, he might have used longer sentences, substituting colons and semicolons for periods to achieve a clearer suggestion of relationships, in this manner:

> Conscience, as the word indicates, is consciousness. It is a specific kind of consciousness: moral awareness, an inner sense of right and wrong. And it is an awareness that has compelling power: we feel bound by it; it commands us; if we disobey it, we feel remorse or anxiety.

Nor are those two examples the only ways the paragraph could be punctuated. Here are two more involving slight changes in wording.

> Conscience (as the word indicates) is consciousness, a specific kind of consciousness. Moral awareness. An inner sense of right and wrong. And it is an awareness that has compelling power—we feel bound by it, it commands us, we feel remorse or anxiety if we disobey it.

> Conscience, as the word indicates, is a specific kind of consciousness —an inner sense of right and wrong, a moral awareness with compelling power to bind and command us, and to make us feel remorse or anxiety if we disobey it.

---

[41] Mortimer Adler, *Great Ideas from The Great Books* (New York: Simon & Schuster, Washington Square Press, Inc., 1961), p. 68.

35. Tone

Tone is the mood of a piece of writing, the type and level of emotional intensity revealed by the writer's choice of words, types of assertions, and structure. The tone suggests the writer's attitude toward his subject and audience. Selecting the most appropriate tone for a piece of writing is important, for an inappropriate tone can elicit an undesired response from the reader. Similarly, keeping the tone consistent, unless there is good reason for shifting, adds to the coherence of the writing. In each of the following suggestions, one type of tone is said to be preferred over another in most cases. This does not necessarily mean that there are no situations in which the unpreferred tone is desirable. Unless otherwise specified, it means that such situations are relatively few, and therefore that we should use that tone only after we have carefully weighed the effects of its use.

a) The *objective* tone, in which the evidence is not heavily colored by the writer's feelings, is preferable to the *subjective*, in which it is.[42] The inclusion of the writer's feelings and attitudes does not, of course, make the tone subjective; it is their dominance or pervasive influence over everything else that does.

b) The *impersonal* tone, in which the reader is not addressed directly, is preferable to the *personal*, in which he is. Unless the "you" reference to the reader is demanded by the occasion, it is distracting, even offensive.

c) The *requesting* or *urging* tone is preferable to the *imploring* or *demanding*. Many situations require the writer to request a particular line of action. Some even require a strong request. But few require him to resort to begging, which suggests (correctly or incorrectly) that his emotional anxiety has displaced his rationality, or to demanding, which is as likely to inspire resistance as compliance.

d) The *ironic* tone is preferable to the *sarcastic*. Both irony and sarcasm involve saying one thing and meaning the opposite, but the purpose of irony is to show the complex or near-contradictory nature of some reality or the contrast between the expected and

---

[42] Of course, in cases where the writer for some good reason chooses to have his feelings pervade the piece, the subjective tone would be preferable.

the actual; and the purpose of sarcasm is to mock or ridicule someone or something.

The term "tone" also refers to the writer's attitude toward himself in relation to his subject. If we say the tone of a piece of writing is *omniscient*, we mean that the writer's choice of words, types of assertions, and structure suggest that he regards himself as knowing everything about the subject. Because such knowledge is clearly inconsistent with the human condition it always suggests that since the writer has apparently committed a fundamenal error in his view of himself, he is likely to be less than accurate in his view of any other subject. For this reason the omniscient tone is always counterproductive and therefore always ineffective with an intelligent audience.

Avoiding a tone of omniscience is part of the larger problem of knowing when to be forceful, when to suggest, when to leave the question open. One of the most common tendencies of nonprofessional (also, unfortunately, of some professional) writers is to cover lack of understanding of an issue with a show of force. It seldom impresses the critical reader who sees it for what it is: a sometimes dishonest, always empty cover for ignorance. We can and should speak unequivocally when we are stating a fact, or a belief based on some significant evidence that we have taken time to evaluate. But when our evidence is slight or relatively insignificant or when we have not evaluated it carefully—and certainly when it may be interpreted in more than one way—we should be careful *merely to suggest* the conclusion as a *possible* one.

Here are two examples of effective forceful statements, the first supported by fact, the second by significant evidence carefully evaluated:

> a) In your editorial of June 30, you stated that two hundred students demonstrated at this college on the evening of June 29. *This figure is incorrect.* I participated in the demonstration. Some students came late and others left early, so the number involved fluctuated throughout the evening. *But at no time did the number exceed fifty.* This fact is supported by the June 30 news stories in two other area papers—The Gardville *Clarion* and The Ashby *Times*—whose estimates of students involved were forty-five and thirty, respectively.

> b) No fewer than ten students testified that John was not in the building when the false alarm occurred. Among those testifying

were the President of the Student Senate, the Student Union President, and two dormitory proctors, all of whom were attending a movie with John when the incident occurred. *It is absurd to set this evidence aside and charge him with the violation* because he committed a similar offense last year and because two students saw someone who "looked very much like John" lingering by the alarm box just before the incident. *This charge is an insult to the integrity of the ten witnesses, to the most basic concepts of legal justice, and to the intelligence of the entire campus community.*

In the next example the subject was the displacement of workers by automation. The writer raised the question of whether some workers displaced by machines might be employed at jobs that "ought to be done," but are not being done, jobs such as auxiliary police protection, beautification of highways and landscapes, assistance to educators. But since the subject is a complex one, and the number of workers that could be used efficiently in such work is not known, the writer was careful not to be too conclusive or forceful in presenting his idea, but rather to suggest it.

We are not suggesting that there are enough jobs of this kind to take up the slack caused by automation and thus solve the problem of unemployment. Our proposal is more modest; we only say that automation creates an opportunity as well as a problem. It gives us the chance to make the Great Society a gracious society as well as a merely prosperous one.

Achieving the Gracious Society would require rethinking some of our assumptions about how services should be paid for. If decent and adequately manned public transportation "costs too much," inasmuch as it cannot support itself by the fares it charges, could we not consider subsidizing it? Could we not figure out ways of putting the unskilled unemployed to work in socially useful services by carrying part of their salaries as a social cost rather than charging them wholly to individual enterprises? These are not easy questions to answer. But they are worth trying to answer for the sake of the Gracious Society that America could be.[43]

Notice that while in the first paragraph the writer suggested one possible partial solution, in the second paragraph he merely raised some questions that should be asked. We must never feel that by suggesting or by merely raising questions we are being ineffective. There is a place for force, a place for suggestion, and a place for raising questions. Effectiveness lies in using the one appropriate to our composition.

[43] Editorial in *America*, March 27, 1965, p. 416.

36.   Exaggeration vs. Understatement

Exaggeration is usually a serious fault. A perceptive reader may overlook in a writer an occasional lapse of moderation, particularly if it is clearly done for effect. But when a writer yields to it more than infrequently, the reader loses confidence in him. (We subtract mentally as many points from a golfer's score today as we caught him adding yesterday.) If we would gain and keep our reader's confidence, we should avoid exaggeration. Before we say a film is the "best" or the "worst" we have ever seen, we should consider the possibility that it is just plain "good" or "bad." If every situation we discuss is a "dire" situation, every danger to our country the "ultimate" danger, every crime the "vilest" and "most despicable," every struggle a "key" struggle, then none of these things is very important.

If we feel it is not enough to be accurate in our appraisal, then we should tend toward *under*statement. For understatement shows a sense of proportion, a balance and calmness, the qualities that win a reader's confidence, the very qualities that keep a writer from exaggerating. Observe the difference in these statements:

Exaggeration	*Understatement*
The task of getting pledges for our fraternity will be herculean.	The task of establishing a colony on the moon will not be easy.
That play was the most boring, least relevant play I have ever seen.	I have seen less boring, more relevant plays.

37.   Place of Self

The primary purpose in any nonfiction writing is to call attention to an idea or an experience or a feeling. It is to reveal what the writer has done, seen heard about or thought—*not who he is*. Therefore, whenever, a writer lets his "presence" in a piece of writing take precedence over his purpose—whenever he repeats *I, me, mine, my, myself,* to the point of the reader's distraction—he diverts his reader's attention from his idea and defeats his own purpose.

A helpful rule is to keep ourselves out of our writing unless doing so makes it stilted or awkward. There are, of course, times when we have to be "present" in the writing; for example, in first person extended illustration. But even then our presence should be as limited as possible. Notice how obtrusive the writer's presence is in the paragraph below, and how much more effective his description is in the revision.

Original	*Revision*
I was eating my lunch in the college snack bar when I saw him enter carrying his tray. I found his appearance shocking. I saw that he was bare-chested and shoeless. By now I had stopped eating. I closed my eyes for a moment and then looked again to be sure I had not imagined him. As I looked closer I saw that his head was clean-shaven, and that he wore denim pants cut off at the knee. I watched as he found a table and turned around to sit down. Then came my biggest shock. I saw tattooed on his back in large letters, "I AM AN INDIVIDUAL."	I was eating my lunch in the college snack bar when he entered carrying his tray. He was bare-chested and shoeless. I stopped eating, closed my eyes for a moment, then looked again to be sure I had not imagined him. His head was clean-shaven, and he wore denim pants cut off at the knee. He found a table and turned around to sit down, revealing the biggest shock. On his back was tattooed in large letters, "I AM AN INDIVIDUAL."

38. Revising

If there is a single way to achieve excellence in writing, it is surely by revising every line that does not read well. In a very real sense, *writing is rewriting*. Even the professional writer, who writes several hours each day, seldom expresses his thoughts as he wishes to in the first draft. While he is writing, he develops new ideas, new approaches. The process of expressing a view suggests the inadequacy of the view, and he proceeds to reexamine and revise it. The "effortlessness" of professional writing is achieved with great effort. The idea that gifted writers don't have to labor over their work is an illusion that survives only because readers are permitted to see the result of the labor and not the labor itself. James Thurber once told an interviewer about his wife's negative reaction to the first draft of a piece he was writing (she called it "high-school stuff"). In explaining his reply to her, he commented on his need to rewrite:

I have to tell her to wait until the seventh draft, it'll work out all right. I don't know why that should be so, that the first or second draft of everything I write reads as if it was turned out by a charwoman. I've only written one piece quickly. I wrote a thing called "File and Forget" in one afternoon—but only because it was a series of letters just as one would ordinarily dictate. And I'd have to admit that the last letter of the series, after doing all the others that one afternoon, took me a week. It was the end of the piece and I had to fuss over it.[44]

Of course, few of us who are not full-time professional writers can afford the time necessary to write seven drafts of anything— even though in most cases our writing has greater need of polish. The best we can do is to write and revise as efficiently as possible, in order to make the best use of our limited time. The following suggestions can help us to become more efficient:

a) Keep the rough draft rough.[45] Don't dawdle over style or organization. Pay no attention to errors in grammar and usage, improper punctuation, faulty paragraphing, the absence of transitions, and so on. Write it quickly. It is much easier to change something that is already written, however badly written it may be, than to perfect each part as you write it. Similarly, never look up the spelling or meaning of a word while writing the rough draft. Time spent looking up a word in a sentence that may be deleted from the final draft is time wasted.

b) If possible, don't evaluate the rough draft immediately after it is finished. Wait a few days or at least a few hours: you'll tend to see it more objectively then. Evaluate its substance, organization, and style in light of your idea, purpose, and audience. Consult the appropriate parts of this text, as necessary. Don't be afraid to make radical changes, if you feel they will improve the composition. If some parts do not fit, throw them out; if a certain idea is underdeveloped, develop it further; if the focus is not clear, do whatever is necessary to sharpen it; add transitions where they are needed, and so on. (Remember that not every part of the composition will require the same amount of attention. Some parts of the first draft may require no revision at all—others, particularly those including

[44] James Thurber in Malcolm Cowley, ed., *Writers at Work* (New York: The Viking Press, Inc., 1958), p. 88.

[45] An idea outline may, of course, precede the rough draft. The decision whether or not to outline depends partly on the complexity of the subject and proposed length of treatment, and partly on individual preference. Some writers work best from an outline; others do not feel the need for one.

one of the techniques of analysis, may require three or four revisions.) When you have completed these revisions, find and correct all errors in grammar and usage, and type or write the final draft. If you type it, be sure to proofread for typing errors.

c) Remember that the wise writer learns his own strengths and weaknesses in writing. Perhaps he organizes well but tends to write in a flat, lifeless style. Or perhaps his style is clear and varied, but he tends to leave thoughts undeveloped and to omit transitions. Whatever his weakness may be, he makes certain to address it in his revision. In writing there is no shame in having a weakness, but only in refusing to acknowledge and deal with it.

4

A Glossary of Grammar and Usage

How important is it for us to observe the conventions of grammar and usage? Less important than some teachers have at times believed or seemed to believe, and more important than many students believe. The conventions of grammar and usage do not in themselves constitute writing excellence. A piece of writing can be completely free of mechanical errors and yet be very ineffective. However, the conventions are not without value. Every time we observe them, we smooth the path to the reader's understanding of our message. Every time we violate them, we distract him or place an obstacle in the way of his understanding. Therefore, the observance of the conventions of grammar and usage is a rhetorical imperative.

The following is a brief list of common problems in grammar and usage. Many of the entries involve very fundamental points. These are included because even the most competent student writers frequently have one or two "pet" errors and many more need an occasional reminder about distinctions they have forgotten. For fuller treatment of the entries listed here and of related matters, there is, of course, no substitute for a good dictionary.

G1. ABBREVIATIONS

Abbreviations should generally be avoided in formal writing. However, there are several exceptions to this rule: forms of designation or address—St. Francis, Mr. Jones, Mrs. Brown; titles—Edgar Swensen, M.D., Charles Cook, B.A., M.A., Ph.D.; references to time—8:00 A.M., 10:20 P.M., 1965 A.D.

G2.   ACCEPT, EXCEPT

Accept is a verb meaning "to take willingly." *Except* is a preposition meaning "but"

Right   I *accept* your invitation.

Right   Everyone was in class *except* Bill.

G3.   ADJECTIVE, ADVERB

An adjective modifies a noun or pronoun. An adverb modifies a verb, an adjective, or another adverb. Never use an adjective in place of an adverb. For example:

Wrong   He plays poker *good*.   (*Good*, an adjective, cannot modify the verb *plays*.)

Right   He plays poker *well*.

Right   He is a *good* poker player.   (Here *good* modifies the noun "player.")

Often the adjective and adverb forms of a word differ only in that the adverb form has a final *-ly*. For example, *real* and *really; efficient, efficiently*. In some cases, however, the two forms are identical. For example, *fast* is both the adjective and the adverb form. If you are unsure whether a particular word is an adjective or adverb form, consult your dictionary.

G4.   AFFECT, EFFECT

Affect means "to influence." *Effect* as a verb means "to cause"; as a noun, "a result."

Right   The experience will *affect* my outlook on life.

Right   The doctor can *effect* a cure. (verb)

Right   The *effect* was tragic. (noun)

G5.   AGREEMENT

Subjects and verbs should always agree in number. A singular subject takes a singular form of the verb; a plural subject, a plural form.

Right	John was doing well before the exam.
Right	I was doing well before the exam.
Wrong	John and I was doing well before the exam. ("John and I" represents two people and therefore demands the plural form *were*.)
Wrong	Every Saturday she invite me to dinner. ("She" represents one person and therefore demands the singular form of the verb, *invites*. Don't be confused by the fact that a final *s* denotes plural in most nouns, but third person singular in present tense verbs—"he goes," "she writes," "it smells.")

Words that clearly represent *one* person, place, or thing always take the singular form of the verb. The most common of these words are *anyone* (*-body*), *anyplace, anything; everyone* (*-body*), *every place, everything; someone* (*-body*), *someplace, something.*

Right	Is anyone here of Polish descent?
Right	Everything was in order.
Right	Someplace there is a girl for Herb.

The expressions "either . . . or" and "neither . . . nor" also take the singular form of the verb, unless the second noun they express is plural.

Right	Either pie or ice cream is tonight's desert.
Right	Neither my car nor my father's runs well.
Wrong	Neither Dan nor his brothers is permitted to attend out-of-town dances. (The second noun, "brothers," is plural. Therefore the plural form of the verb, "are permitted," should be used.)

G6. ALLOT, A LOT

Allot is a verb meaning "to distribute or apportion." *A lot,* always written as two words, means "much."

G7. ALREADY, ALL READY

Already means "before that time." But *all ready* means "completely prepared" ("all set" in colloquial usage).

Right	He was *already* there where she arrived.
Right	He was *all ready* to leave when the phone rang.

G8.   ALTOGETHER, ALL TOGETHER

Altogether means "entirely," "completely," *All together* means "everyone at the same time" or "with one another," and is usually separated by other words.

Right   It was an *altogether* wasted evening.

Right   We *all* went to the picnic *together*.

G9.   ALWAYS, ALL WAYS

Always means "all the time," "forever." *All ways* means "every method," and is often separated by another word or words.

Right   I'll *always* love you.

Right   We tried *all* lawful *ways* to obtain the book.

G10.   ARE, OUR

Are is a part of the verb "to be." *Our* is a possessive pronoun.

Right   They *are* arriving at noon.

Right   *Our* car is in the garage.

G11.   BESIDE, BESIDES

Beside means "next to." *Besides* means "anyway" or "moreover."

Right   Sally sits *beside* me in class.

Right   I was too tired to go. *Besides,* I had work to do.

G12.   BETWEEN, AMONG

Use *between* when two persons, places, or things are involved; *among* when more than two.

Right   The most grueling competition was *between* John and me.

Right   The prize money was divided *among* the five who finished the race first.

G13.   CAN, MAY

Can concerns ability to do something; *may* concerns permission to. Thus, "I know I *can* do better work if I try," and "Mother, *may* I borrow five dollars?" are both correct. (An exception to this is a question in which the negative form of the expression is used: "Why can't I go out tomorrow night?" is preferable to "Why may I not go out tomorrow night?" because it is less awkward.)

G14. CAPITALIZATION

Capitalize the initial letter of the first word in a sentence; the pronoun "I"; people's names and their titles, when the titles are used to refer specifically to them; the names of countries, states, regions, cities, and towns; names of the Deity and the titles of sacred writings; names of races and nationalities, religious denominations, schools and colleges, business establishments, organizations and members of organizations; names of periods of history, the days of the week, the months (but not the seasons), holidays; names of special events; titles of specific courses of study; titles of published or produced works, including plays and films (excluding *a, an, the,* and prepositions and conjunctions of fewer than five letters).

G15. CENSOR, CENSER, CENSURE

Censor as a verb means "to examine that which may be objectionable and, if it is, to suppress it"; as a noun, "the official who examines and suppresses." *Censer* is a noun meaning "a vessel containing incense, usually used in worship." *Censure* as a verb means "to disapprove, blame, or condemn"; as a noun, "the expression of disapproval, blame, or condemnation."

Right   Let us hope no one *censors* the book.

Right   The *censor* is a personable man, but his intelligence is limited.

Right   The altar boy filled the *censer* with incense.

Right   No one stepped forward to *censure* her.

Right   Everyone suspected him, but somehow he escaped *censure.*

G16. CHOOSE, CHOSE

Both words are forms of the same verb—*to choose. Choose* is a present tense form and *chose* is the past tense form. (*Choose* rhymes with *news, chose* with *toes.*)

Right   *Choose* your major.

Right   He *chose* history.

G17. CLICHÉS

Clichés are overused or "tired" expressions which, because of their familiarity to most readers, make our writing dull and boring. Always prefer fresh, original phrasing to clichés such as the following:

true blue
fit as a fiddle
gentle as a lamb
shoulder to the wheel
nose to the grindstone
eye on the ball
his heart in his work

G18. COLLOQUIALISMS

Colloquialisms are expressions that are acceptable in informal writing and conversation but *unacceptable* in formal. For example, "I'm bushed" instead of "I'm exhausted," "cop" instead of "policeman."

G19. COMMA SPLICE

A comma splice is the incorrect use of a comma to mark a full stop, frequently causing the reader to falter.

Wrong   Most of the members of my fraternity bowl for relaxation, I play golf.

Right   Most of the members of my fraternity bowl for relaxation, but I play golf.

Right   Most of the members of my fraternity bowl for relaxation. I play golf.

Substituting a dash, a colon, or a semicolon for the period in the above sentence would also be acceptable.

G20. CONSCIENCE, CONSCIOUS

Conscience is a noun meaning "inner moral guide," "sense of right and wrong in ethical matters." *Conscious* is an adjective meaning "mentally awake" or "aware."

Right   "Let your *conscience* be your guide."

Right   He was *conscious* (mentally awake) when he arrived at the hospital.

Right   We must be *conscious* (aware) of our responsibilities as citizens.

G21. DANGLING MODIFIER

A dangling modifier is a clause or phrase expressed in such a way that its relationship to the rest of the sentence is unclear or misleading.

Dangling   After boiling for thirty minutes, broil the chicken until it is golden brown. (What is to be boiled, the cook or the chicken?)

Clear   After boiling the chicken for thirty minutes, broil it until it is golden brown.

G22. DIFFERENT FROM, DIFFERENT THAN

When you are speaking of a difference between two people, places, or things, use *different from*. When you are speaking of a difference in the same person, place, or thing over a period of time, use *different than*.

Right   John's idea of a good time is *different from* mine.

Right   His political convictions are *different* today *than* they were three years ago.

G23. DINER, DINNER

Diner means "an informal restaurant" or "one who dines." *Dinner* means "the main meal of the day." (*Diner* rhymes with *finer*, *dinner* with *winner*.)

G24. EACH OTHER, ONE ANOTHER

Use *each other* when referring to *two people*, *one another* when referring to *more than two people*.

Right   I've never seen a husband and wife so devoted to *each other* as Sam and Sue.

Right   Women were climbing over *one another* at the sale counters.

G25.   ETC, &

Etc. is an abbreviation of the Latin *et cetera*, which means "and others" or "and so forth"; & is a symbol used in place of "and." Although both are widely used in informal writing, they are still considered unacceptable in formal writing.

G26.   FARTHER, FURTHER

Use *farther* when referring to *distance*, further when referring to *degree*.

Right   It's *farther* from here to my home than to yours.

Right   He gets *further* into debt each week.

G27.   FAULTY COMPARISON

A faulty comparison does not compare what the writer intends to compare.

Faulty   Unlike high school, the college student devotes many hours to studying.

Correct   Unlike *the high school student, the college student* devotes many hours to studying.

G28.   FAULTY DEFINITION

A definition expresses *what* something is or means. It proceeds from the general class to which the thing belongs to its individual characteristics. Thus, "A democracy is that form of government . . ." and "Gravity is a force that . . ." Never begin a definition with *when* or *why*: for example, never say "A democracy is *when* . . ." or "Gravity is *why*. . . ."

G29.   FAULTY REFERENCE

A faulty reference does not refer to what the writer intends to refer.

Faulty   When a man obtains his goal in life, such as the *president* of a company, we say he is successful.

Correct   When a man obtains his goal in life, such as the *presidency* of a company, we say he is successful.

G30. HEAR, HERE

These words sound alike. But hear is a *verb*, and *here* is an *adverb* indicating place.

Right   I *hear* your sister singing.
Right   *Here* is where the old church once stood.

G31. IMMORAL, AMORAL

Immoral means "not conforming to a moral code one endorses in theory." *Amoral* means "not having a moral code."

G32. HEALTHY, HEALTHFUL

Healthy means "in good health" or "conducive to health in an indirect or figurative sense." *Healthful* means "nutritious," "health-producing in a direct, literal sense."

Right   He is a *healthy* boy. ("in good health")
Right   This is a *healthy* climate. (conducive to health in an indirect sense")
Right   The food served in our dining hall is *healthful*.

G33. ILLITERACIES

Illiteracies are errors in grammar and usage which are characteristically made by the uneducated. The following are common examples:

Illiteracy	*Correct Expression*
ain't	am not
aren't I	am I not
awful good	very good

("Awful" means "extremely bad"; therefore, "awful good" is a contradiction.)

can't hardly	can hardly

("*Hardly* means "barely"; therefore, to say "can't hardly" means "cannot barely," which makes no sense. Similarly, "couldn't hardly" is an illiteracy.)

could of	could have

("Of" is a preposition. It cannot substitute for the helping verb "have." Similarly, "should of," "may of," "might of," are illiteracies.)

hisself	himself
irregardless	regardless

(The prefix *ir-* and the suffix *-less* both mean "without"; therefore *irregardless* is a redundancy.)

so don't I	so do I

("So don't I" says the opposite of what is meant. Similarly, "so won't I" is an illiteracy.)

theirselves	themselves

G34. ILLUSION, ALLUSION

Illusion means "a false idea or impression" or "that which creates such an impression." *Allusion* means "a casual reference to a person, place or thing."

Right   He is fond of the *illusion* that life will make no demands upon him.

Right   Her *allusion* to Lincoln's Gettysburg address was irrelevant to the issue.

G35. IMPLY, INFER

Imply means "to suggest indirectly" or "to hint at." *Infer* means "to judge or conclude."

Right   You seem to *imply* that I am at fault.

Right   Both writers *infer* that the situation is hopeless.

G36. INCOMPLETE COMPARISON

A comparison is incomplete whenever we do not specify both what we are comparing and what we are comparing it with. If we say, "A person who lives in an atmosphere of violence is more apt to be violent," we have left open the question, "More apt to be violent than who or what?" "This is a better toothpaste" leaves open the question, "Better than what?" "Better than it was yesterday?" or "Better than some other toothpaste?"

G37. ITS, IT'S

Its is a possessive pronoun. *It's* is the contraction of "it is."

Right   The elephant raised *its* trunk and trumpeted.
Right   *It's* a beautiful day.

G38. JARGON

Jargon sometimes means technical terminology and phrasing. More often it means unnecessarily involved, unintelligible phrasing. For example, "for the purpose of" instead of "for," "with respect to" instead of "about," "in the event that" for "if." (See *Simplicity* in "Other Elements of Rhetoric.")

G39. LAY, LIE

These words are both verbs. *Lay* means *to place or put.*

Present Tense	lay	I *lay* the book on the desk.
Past Tense	laid	Yesterday I *laid* the book on my desk.
Present Perfect	have laid	I *have laid* the books on my dresser.

Lie means *to rest or recline.*

Present Tense	lie	I *lie* down for a nap every afternoon at 1:00 P.M.
Past Tense	lay	I *lay* down yesterday morning.
Present Perfect	have lain	I *have lain* down very frequently because I am ill.

G40. LEAD, LED

Lead can be used in two ways—as a present tense form of the verb *to lead* (rhymes with *seed*); as a noun meaning a type of metal (rhymes with *head*). But *led* (also rhymes with *head*) is the past tense form of the verb *to lead.*

Right   No one can *lead* the group as forcefully as Ralph.
Right   The safe is lined with *lead.*
Right   Ralph has *led* the group for five years.

G41. LEAVE, LET

Leave means "to depart or to cause to remain." *Let* means "to permit."

Right   *Leave* this house immediately.
Right   He wished to *leave* his clothes here.
Right   *Let* me carry that package.

G42. LESS, FEWER

Less means "to a smaller extent or degree" or "in a smaller size or degree." *Fewer* means "smaller in *number*." Use *fewer* whenever you are referring to people, places, or things which are separate units.

Right   Less money, less butter, less pride, less patriotism, less value.

Right   Fewer dollars, fewer cars, fewer trees, fewer people, fewer pins.

G43. LIKE, AS

Although contemporary usage has somewhat blurred the distinction between these words in some constructions, most educated people avoid substituting *like* for *as* when the meaning intended is "in the same manner or way that." For example, "It tasted quite good, like a breakfast food should" would be unacceptable in formal writing. (Consult a good dictionary to learn the numerous uses of each word.)

G44. LOOSE, LOSE

Loose means "unattached" or "free from restraint." *Lose* means "to misplace or be deprived of." (*Loose* rhymes with *goose*, *lose* with *blues*.)

Right   The cow is *loose*.
Right   Did you *lose* your pen?

G45. MANY, MUCH

Many means "a large number of individual units." *Much* means "a large quantity of something not usually considered in individual units."

Right   Many people, many typewriters, many houses, many countries, many bananas.

Right   Much coffee, much pride, much ignorance, much corn, much love.

G46. MAYBE, MAY BE

These expressions have essentially the same meaning. But *maybe* is an *adverb* and *may be* is a *verb* form (verb *to be* plus its auxiliary *may*). Which you use depends on the part of speech your sentence calls for.

Wrong   *May be* I'll go to the movies.

Right   *Maybe* I'll go to the movies.

Wrong   This *maybe* our only chance.

Right   This *may be* our only chance.

G47. ME, I

Me is the objective case of the personal pronoun *I*. The most common error with these words is using *I* instead of *me* as the object of a preposition.

Wrong   You'll have to choose between John and *I*

Right   You'll have to choose between John and *me*.

G48. MISPLACED MODIFIER

The placement of a word, phrase, or clause often determines the meaning conveyed. Be sure to place all phrases and clauses where they will convey the exact meaning you intend.

Only you can eat at that table. (No one else can eat there.)

You can eat *only* at that table. (You can eat at no other table.)

The man *standing over there* paid us for the fish we caught. (The man is standing over there.)

The man paid us for the fish we caught *standing over there*. (We were standing over there when we caught the fish.)

G49. MIXED CONSTRUCTION

Mixed construction is the error of beginning a sentence with one grammatical structure and then shifting to another.

Wrong   By doing it this way is the fastest way to achieve our goal.

Right   By doing it this way we can achieve our goal most quickly.

Right   Doing it this way is the fastest way to achieve our goal.

G50.   MORAL, MORALE

Moral refers to right conduct or the difference between right and wrong. *Morale* refers to a person's mental state, his degree of confidence, cheerfulness, enthusiasm.

Right   He is a very *moral* person.
Right   The soldiers' *morale* is high.

G51.   MORE, MOST

More, or the word ending *-er* that often substitutes for it, (as in *smoothe*r) is used in comparing two people, places, or things. *Most,* or the word ending *-est* that often substitutes for it, is used to denote the highest degree. *More* is *never* used together with *-er,* nor is *most* with *-est.*

Right   Jane is *more* cautious than Sally.
Right   Sally is *prettier* than Jane.
Right   He is the *most* obstinate person I have ever met.
Right   Professor Smith's course is the easi*est* one I have this term.
Wrong   I am more kind*er* than my brother.
Wrong   My neighbors are the *most* pleasant*est* people in town.

G52.   MOST, ALMOST

Most means "the highest degree." *Almost* means "nearly."

Right   He is the *most* handsome boy on the team.
Right   Your car is *almost* finished, sir.

G53.   NEEDLESS SEPARATION OF RELATED WORDS

Related words should never be needlessly separated by long phrases or clauses. Short parenthetical expressions may be placed between them but only when the gain in variety or rhythm outweighs the added difficulty in reading.

Wrong   Edward, anxious to get home in time for the television show, exceeded the speed limit.
Right   Anxious to get home in time for the television show, Edward exceeded the speed limit.
Right   We cannot say, however, that he should be praised.

G54. NICE, SWELL, FINE, GOOD, WELL

Avoid using these words in place of more specific ones. They are usually too vague to be meaningful.

G55. NUMBER, AMOUNT

Use *number* when referring to persons or places or things usually considered as individual units. Use *amount* when referring to things not usually considered individual units.

Right	a number of people, a number of towns, a number of birds, a number of tools.
Right	an amount of money, an amount of violence, an amount of wheat.

G56. NUMBERS

In formal writing write out all numbers which can be expressed in one or two words. Use figures for all others. If, however, you are mentioning several numbers, one or more of which would require more than two words, use figures for all.

Right	one hundred dollars, thirteen million dollars, thirty-eight cents.
Right	$3,025, $14.83, $250,000.
Right	John spent $50, Harry $40, and Bill $137.50.

G57. OMISSION OF NECESSARY WORDS

When you proofread your writing, always check to be sure you haven't omitted words necessary to complete or clarify your meaning.

Omission	Thank you for your of August 9.
Correction	Thank you for your *letter* of August 9.
Omission	On our farm we have a pig, some cows, dog, and three horses.
Correction	On our farm we have a pig, some cows, *a* dog, and three horses.

G58. PASSED, PAST

Passed is a verb form. *Past* as an adjective means "gone by, ended"; as a noun, "that time which no longer is."

Right   The car *passed* us at the turn.
Right   The *past* week was hectic.
Right   It is foolish to think only of the *past.*

G59. PERSONAL, PERSONNEL

Personal (pronounced PER-son-al) means "private." *Personnel* (pronounced per-son-NEL) means "employees" as a noun, and "pertaining to employees" as an adjective.

Right   The letter's contents are *personal.*
Right   All *personnel* of the bank are required to attend the meeting.
Right   That company has no clearly defined *personnel* policy.

G60. PLURALS

Be sure to use the plural form of a noun when you intend a plural meaning.

Right   The Communists have infiltrated the group.

G61. PRINCIPAL, PRINCIPLE

Principal as a noun means "the chief administrative officer of a school"; as an adjective, "main or primary." *Principle* is a noun meaning "rule."

Right   The *principal* spoke to the students at their graduation.
Right   The *principal* reason I am in college is to learn.
Right   It is an important *principle* of rhetoric.

G62. PROPOSE, PURPOSE

Propose is a verb meaning "to offer or suggest." *Purpose* is a noun meaning "reason or intention."

Right   I *propose* we eliminate this item from the budget.
Right   Our *purpose* in being here is no secret.

G63. PROVIDED, PROVIDING

Provided means "cared for" or "with the provision that." *Providing* means "furnishing."

Right   He *provided* well for his family.
Right   We may go *provided* our work is done.
Wrong   We may go *providing* our work is done.
Right   She was responsible for *providing* the salads for the picnic.

G64. QUITE, QUIET

Quite is a one-syllable word that rhymes with "bite." *Quiet* is a two-syllable word that rhymes with "diet." *Quite* means "rather"; *quiet*, "silent."

Right   They are *quite* concerned about his strange behavior.
Right   John, be *quiet*.

G65. RESPECTFULLY, RESPECTIVELY

Respectfully means "with respect." *Respectively* means "pertaining to what has preceded, and in the same order."

Right   Treat your elders *respectfully*.
Right   Tom, Herb, and Helen went to Florida, New York, and Arizona, *respectively*.

G66. RISE, RAISE

Rise means "to get up or go up." *Raise* means "to cause to rise."

Right   I *rise* at the same time every day.
Right   Watch the balloons *rise*.
Right   I'm not sure they can *raise* the sunken ship.

G67. RUN-ON SENTENCE

A run-on sentence is a sentence in which two or more independent clauses are fused together without the necessary punctuation. "I am a lucky person I won a turkey last Thanksgiving and now I've won a new car" lacks necessary punctuation (in this case a period or colon) between "person" and "I."

G68. SENT, CENT, SCENT

Sent is a form of the verb *to send*. *Cent* means "penny." *Scent* means "odor."

Right   He was *sent* to jail.

Right   It cost one *cent*.

Right   That *scent* is very fragrant.

G69. SENTENCE FRAGMENT

A sentence fragment is an incomplete expression. Some fragments are stylistically effective—that is, they add force or variety to the writing. Others are awkward and therefore ineffective.

Effective   "I don't want to go to the movies with you. I don't want to go to the movies with anyone. I want to be alone. Alone." ("Alone" is a fragment, but it adds force to the passage without being awkward.)

Effective   "You can overcome these obstacles to effective expression and learn to speak and write clearly, gracefully, movingly. But only if you will work." ("But only if you will work" is a fragment, but it adds force to the passage without being awkward.)

Awkward   "Although I wanted very much to go to the theater. My mother made me stay home." (The first clause is awkward when set off by itself. It depends too much on the second. It should be written, "Although I wanted very much to go to the theater, my mother made me stay home.")

G70. SIGHT, SITE, CITE

Sight refers to vision, viewing, or that which is viewed. *Site* is "a location, often a building location." And *cite* means "to make reference to" or "to credit."

Right   What a beautiful *sight* that valley is in autumn.

Right   Can you *sight* the artillery

Right   This is the *site* of the new garage.

Right   We are supposed to *cite* all our references.

G71. SINCE, SENSE (SENCE)

Since means "from a former time to now." *Sense* as a verb means "to perceive or feel intuitively"; as a noun, "the relative quality of one's judgment" or "one of the means of sensory perception." *Sence* is an incorrect form sometimes substituted for either *since* or *sense*.

Right   I haven't been able to sleep *since* the accident.
Right   He could *sense* that something was wrong.
Right   Have the good *sense* to avoid him in the future.
Right   My *sense* of taste has been dulled by the garlic.

G72. SIT, SET

Both words are verbs. But *sit* means "to rest or recline" and *set* means "to place or put."

Present Tense	sit	I always *sit* down when I teach.
Past Tense	sat	She *sat* down quickly.
Present Perfect	have sat	They *have sat* there every day this week.
Present Tense	set	*Set* the chair there.
Past Tense	set	The moving men *set* it there.
Present Perfect	have set	I *have set* it where you said.

G73. SLANG

Slang means highly colloquial expressions or uncultivated dialect, unacceptable in formal and most informal writing, except when used in direct quotation from the speech or writing of others—for example, "we cut out fast," "she was a real swinger." Modern "hip" expressions are also a common form of slang—for example, "don't blow your cool."

G74. SO, SOW, SEW

So has a variety of meanings. The principal ones are "in the way indicated," "in order," "in that degree," "very." *Sow* means "to scatter seed on the ground." And *sew* means "to stitch material."

Right   Do it now *so* that you can have this evening free.
Right   He plans to *sow* seed tonight.
Right   Can you *sew* this right away?

G75. SPELLING

Correct spelling depends on the effective interplay of two skills—visualizing how we have seen the word spelled before, and hearing ("sounding out") the parts of the word. Deficiency in either skill can make spelling a problem for us. Since every misspelled word distracts our reader from the thought we are expressing and lessens his confidence in us, it is important that we overcome any spelling problem we may have, no matter how small. There are, of course, no cure-alls for spelling problems. But the following suggestions can be of considerable help:

a) Be more observant as you read: notice how professional writers spell words you have difficulty with; try to remember the correct spellings.

b) Learn the way your dictionary marks syllable divisions and the symbols it uses to distinguish between vowel sounds. (Most dictionaries footnote every page or every other page with a key to pronunciation symbols.) Whenever you look up the spelling of a word, also note exactly how it should be pronounced.

c) Be more meticulous in your speech: pronounce every syllable carefully. Occasionally try to visualize the syllable divisions of words you or others are saying.

d) Make an alphabetical list of words you have difficulty with. Add to it every word you look up. Review the list from time to time, pronouncing each word aloud as you read it. Keep the list handy whenever you write.

G76. STATIONARY, STATIONERY

Stationary means "fixed, not moving." *Stationery* means "writing materials" (paper and envelopes).

G77. THEM, THOSE

Never use *them* in a construction that requires those.

Wrong   *Them* students are unfriendly.
Right   *Those* students are unfriendly.

G78. THEN, THAN

Then indicates time. *Than* introduces the second part of a comparison.

Right   *Then* we went to school.
Right   He is more active *than* I.

G79. THERE, THEIR, THEY'RE

These words are pronounced exactly the same. But *there* is an adverb indicating place, *their* is a pronoun showing possession, and *they're* is a contraction of "they are."

Right   Put the package *there.*
Right   *Their* coats are in the first closet.
Right   *They're* arriving at noon.

G80. THERE IS, THERE ARE

In either expression *there* is never the actual subject, though its position makes it seem to be. The actual subject follows the expression. If that subject is singular, use *is;* if plural, *are.*

Right   There *is* one *girl* in the class who raises her hand for every question. (The subject *girl* is singular; therefore *is* is the correct word.)

Right   There *are* several *cars* in town that resemble mine. (The subject *cars* is plural; therefore *are* is the correct word.)

G81. THROUGH (THRU), THREW

Through means "between" or "in one side and out the other." *Thru* is an unacceptable form of *through. Threw* means "projected or propelled."

Right   The bullet went *through* the deer's neck.
Right   He *threw* his fast ball.

G82. THROUGHOUT, THREW OUT

Throughout means "all during." *Threw out* means "disposed of."

Right   He played in the band *throughout* his college years.
Right   She *threw out* the spoiled food.

G83. TO, TOO

To has many meanings, most of which you are familiar with. But *to* cannot be used as a substitute for *too,* which means "more than enough" or "also."

Right   He gave it *to* me.
Right   I am going *to* wash the dishes.
Right   I am *too* tired to go.
Right   Ask Jim, *too*.

G84. TORTUOUS, TORTUROUS

Tortuous means "twisting, turning, winding, crooked." *Torturous* means "very painful."

Right   The road was so *tortuous* that we had to reduce our speed to twenty miles per hour.
Right   Sitting in his class is a *torturous* experience.

G85. UNACCEPTABLE EXPRESSIONS

Some expressions which are not really illiteracies are nevertheless avoided by most educated people, at least in formal writing.

Unacceptable Expression	*Acceptable Substitute*
alright	all right
awfully good	very good

(*Awfully*, unlike *awful*, has become an acceptable *informal* substitute for "very.")

enthused	enthusiastic
kind of (sort of)	rather (quite)
nauseous	nauseated
the reason is because	the reason is that

(Both *reason* and *because* refer to cause; therefore, "the reason is because" is a redundancy.)

try and	try to
use to be	used to be

G86. UNNECESSARY SHIFT IN PERSON

Unnecessary shift in person is a common type of inconsistency in writing and is very distracting to the reader. For example, a writer will begin speaking of "the student" (third person singular), then shift unnecessarily to "the students" (third person plural), then shift back to "the student," and finally shift to "you" (second person singular or plural). Some shifts, of course, cannot be avoided. If a writer completes an illustration of an incident involving a few students and turns to one involving himself, he must shift from "the students" to "I." This is a *necessary* shift. It is only *un*necessary shifts that should be avoided.

Shifts in person often result from the writer's wish to achieve variety by avoiding repetition of his subject. In such cases, he must be careful to substitute a singular pronoun for a singular noun, a plural pronoun for a plural noun.

Original Subject	*Acceptable Pronoun Substitute*
Jane	she
Ed	he
everyone	he (or she)
the car	it
the cars	they
Ed and Bill	they
John and I	we

G87. UNNECESSARY SHIFT IN TENSE

Like an unnecessary shift in person, this error is a common type of inconsistency that is very distracting to the reader. For example, a writer will begin using past tense—"We *went* to the dance—a few lines later shift unnecessarily to present tense—"We *enter* the dance hall"—and later shift back to past tense—"I *asked* her to dance." A movement from a situation that happened last week to one that is happening now, at the very time the writer is writing, would be a *necessary* shift. It is only *un*necessary shifts in tense that should be avoided.

Similarly, the sequence of tenses should be handled correctly. The following are common errors in tense sequence:

Wrong   *Having been notified* to see my advisor, I *go* to his office.

Right   *Having been notified* to see my advisor, I *went* to his office.

Wrong   Three years *had passed* since I *have seen* him.

Right   Three years *had passed* since I *saw* him.

G88. UNIQUE

Unique means "without parallel, one of a kind." Therefore, the words *more, most,* and *very* shouldn't be used with it.

Wrong	His writing was *more unique* than anyone's.
Right	His writing was *unique*.
Wrong	This experience is *most unique*.
Right	This experience is *unique*.
Wrong	She's a *very unique* girl.
Right	She's a *unique* girl.

G89. WERE, WHERE

Were is a form of the verb "to be"; *where*, an adverb denoting place.

| Right | We *were* the only ones who applauded. |
| Right | Try to remember *where* you left it. |

G90. WHO, WHOM, WHICH, THAT

Who and *whom* are pronouns referring to people. When the word used will be the subject of a verb, use *who*. When the verb already has a subject, use *whom*.

Right	*Who* did you say is coming? (*Who* is the subject of "is coming.")
Right	I spoke to the man *who* sold you the car. (*Who* is the subject of "sold.")
Right	The man *whom* I told you about is here. ("Told" already has a subject— "I.")

Which refers to places and things, never to people.

| Right | This is the town *which* was the scene of the riot. (*Which* refers to "town.") |
| Right | The house *which* was for sale has been sold. (*Which* refers to "house.") |

That refers mainly to places and things but also can refer to people.

Right	Rome is the one city *that* I've always longed to visit. (*That* refers to "city.")
Right	The panther is one animal *that* I'd prefer not to meet at night. (*That* refers to "animal.")
Right	The man *that* stole my wallet is ten dollars richer. (*That* refers to "man.")

G91. WHOEVER, WHOMEVER

This distinction between these two words is the same as that between *who* and *whom*.

Right   *Whoever* speaks to me about it will get a curt reply.
            (*Whoever* is the subject of "speaks.")
Right   You may tell *whomever* you please. (The verbs "may tell" and "please" already have subjects.)

G92. WOMAN, WOMEN

Woman is singular; *women*, plural. Therefore it is correct to say "a *woman*," but incorrect to say "a *women*." This distinction applies as well to other words ending in *-man, men*—for example, *gentleman, gentlemen; freshman, freshmen*.

G93. WORD ENDINGS

Learning to *hear* your writing will help you to avoid omitting word endings.

Wrong   I have *listen* to him long enough.
Right   I have *listened* to him long enough.
Wrong   He fought for what *belong* to him.
Right   He fought for what *belonged* to him.
Wrong   Richard didn't go because of what *happen* before.
Right   Richard didn't go because of what *happened* before.

G94. WRONG DENOTATION

Avoid making denotative errors—using words that do not have the *literal* meaning you intend. For example, do not say, "John is an alchemist" (one who searches for or claims to have found a way to change baser metals into gold) when you mean "John is a chemist," or "He punctured every few words with *um* or *ah*" when you mean "He punctuated every few words with *um* or *ah*."

G95. WRONG CONNOTATION

Avoid making connotative errors—those in which the word is literally correct, but suggests an attitude or association you do not intend. For example, do not say, "He is a remarkable politician" when you mean, "He is a remarkable statesman." ("Politician" suggests a skill in getting votes and in remaining uncommitted on controversial issues.)

G96. YOU, ONE, A PERSON, WE

Traditionally, *you* has been frowned upon in formal writing. *One* has been preferred. For example, the sentence "You don't really know how courageous you are until you are tested," unless it were addressed to a specific person, would have been considered appropriate only in speech or informal writing. Today, though the situation is not exactly reversed, many writers consider *one* too stilted for most writing situations. They prefer *a person* (or a more specific substitute, such as *a man, a woman*). *You* is considered acceptable except where it is obtrusive or too personal to the reader. For many writing situations *we* offers a way to retain the casualness of *you* without becoming personal. There is no clear-cut rule that governs usage in this matter. To decide what is appropriate in a given situation, we must consider the occasion, the audience, and our purpose in writing.

G97. YOUR, YOU'RE

Your is a possessive pronoun. *You're* is a contraction of "you are."

Right   Don't forget *your* coat.
Right   Remember that *you're* in this course to learn.

Index

Reasoning (*cont.*)
  human context (*cont.*)
    syntheses of reality, 2-3
    truths, 4
    validity of ideas, 3-4
    views, 3
    impediments to sound, 5-9, 23:
      absurdity, 7, 8
      assumptions, 6-7
      common sense, 7-8
      error, 7, 8
      ignorance, 7, 8
      oversimplifications, 8-9
      preconceptions, 5-6
      predispositions, 5, 6
      simplifications, 8
      superstitions, 7
    quality of, 22, 24
    recognizing our limitations, 14-17, 23:
      criticism of arguments, 17
      degree of falsity, 16-17
      degree of truth, 16-17
      evidence, 14
      experience, 15
      guessing, 15
      hasty conclusions, 14-15
      knowledge appraisal, 15
      modification of views, 15
      observations, 15
      rejection of false positions, 16
    unmaking our minds, 11-14:
      extension of the idea, 13-14
      reversion of the idea, 12-13
    in writing, 22-23:
      common sense, 23
      contradictions, 23
      drafts, 23
      evidence, 23
      expression, 22
      feeling, 22
      flawed reasoning, 22
      hasty conclusions, 23
      intuition, 23
      main idea, 23
      organization of thoughts, 23, 24
      quality of reasoning, 22, 24
      style, 24
      substance, 24

Reasoning (*cont.*)
  in writing (*cont.*)
    superficialities, 23
    vividness of detail, 22
    writing process, 23
Repetition, 72, 107, 122-23
Reporting, 58-60, 102
Reversion of ideas, 12
Revisions, 136-37
Rhetoric, elements of, 22, 24, 48, 49-138
Rhythm, 107-9:
  awkwardness, 108
  clarity, 107
  clauses, 107
  crispness, 107
  harmony, 107
  melodiousness, 107
  monotony, 107
  phrases, 107, 108
  repetition, 107
  rewriting, 108
  strength, 107
  unity, 109

S

Sarcasm, 28, 132-33
Scope, 49, 88-89, 97:
  analysis, 88
  assertions, 89
  evidence, 88
  explanation, 88
  generalizations, 89
  interpretation, 88
  specificity, degree of, 89
  surface treatment (skimming), 88
Self, the, 135-36
Sensory impressions, 1, 2, 25, 65, 66
Sentences, 52, 107, 112, 113, 115, 116, 117, 130-31
Sequence, 64, 68
Simile, 120
Simplicity, 105-6:
  diction, 105
  in fine writing, 105
  jargon, 106
  obstacles to, 105-6